THE BEST DAMN SALES BOOK EVER

THE BEST DAMN SALES BOOK EVER

16 Rock-Solid Rules for Achieving Sales Success!

WARREN GRESHES

WILEY

John Wiley & Sons, Inc.

Published by John Wiley & Sons, Inc., Hoboken, New Jersey.
Published simultaneously in Canada.

For general information on our other products and services or for technical support,
please contact our Customer Care Department within the United States
at (800) 762-2974, outside the United States at (317) 572-3993 or fax
(317) 572-4002.

Wiley also publishes its books in a variety of electronic formats. Some content that
appears in print may not be available in electronic books. For more information about
Wiley products, visit our web site at www.wiley.com.

Library of Congress Cataloging-in-Publication Data

Greshes, Warren, 1951-
    The best damn sales book ever: 16 rock-solid rules for
achieving sales success / Warren Greshes
        p.   cm.
    Published simultaneously in Canada
    Includes index.
    ISBN-13: 978-0-471-75728-3 (cloth)
    ISBN-10: 0-471-75728-4 (cloth)
    1. Sales personnel—United States.   2. Sales personnel—United
States—Attitudes.   3. Selling.   4. Success in business—United States.
I. Title.
HF5438.25.G736   2006
658.8'1—dc22

                                                    2005026008

Printed in the United States of America.

10   9   8   7

This book is dedicated to my wife Linda,
who at times has had more faith in me than I did,
and to my son Michael and daughter Emily,
who are all part of the answer to the question:

What motivates the motivator?

Contents

Introduction

Being a salesperson is the best job there is. It is one of the few professions in which you can work for someone else and still be working for yourself. It is also one of the only professions where you can work for someone else, make as much money as you want, and not have to beg the boss for a raise.

A salesperson's score is up on the board for all to see, every single day. Nobody can ever tell you you're doing a bad job if you're not. Of course, the down side is: If you're not doing a good job, there's nowhere to run, nowhere to hide. And therein lies the problem.

Most salespeople are not great at what they do. If we looked at every sales organization in the world, we'd find, for the most part, they break down the same way. Ten percent of the salespeople are great; 10 percent should be kicked down the stairs and out the door; and the other 80 percent are merely average.

This book is aimed at two of those groups. The 10 percent at the top, while already successful, are the kind of people who are always looking to get better and can take one good idea and turn it into a veritable gold mine. The middle 80 percent need this book because they need direction. Most of them are mediocre not because they want to be, but because they just don't understand what it takes to be a successful salesperson.

Of course, if those in the bottom 10 percent want to buy this book, I'm not about to stop them. But I'm sure as heck not going to waste a lot of time, energy, and money marketing this book to that group. There's a reason why the bottom 10 percent always seem to remain the bottom 10 percent.

Many sales books focus on some part of the actual sales process—prospecting, closing, referrals, presentation skills, and so on. Others focus on certain psychological or supposedly new ways of selling: customer-centric selling; mirroring and understanding the personality of the customer; relationship selling.

While many of these skills are included in *The Best Damn Sales Book Ever*, this book is about what successful salespeople do to be successful. What makes it unique among sales books is that it starts at the very beginning of the process with the single biggest differentiator between the successful and unsuccessful salesperson: self-motivation.

In fact, this book will teach you how to motivate yourself, by taking you through a process in which you will develop a written five-year plan for your life, career, and business. This five-year plan will enable you to focus more clearly on what you want to accomplish, when you'll accomplish it, and the specific steps you will need to take to accomplish your goals.

Selling is rejection, plain and simple. The top salespeople can deal with it, the rest can't. Ask any sales VP or sales manager and they'll all tell you the same thing. The biggest reason their salespeople do not bring in enough business is that they don't see enough people. They don't see enough people because they fear rejection. They fear rejection because they don't know how much rejection they need. And they don't know how much rejection they need because they don't know what they need or want. They have no goals or plans for their lives, careers, or businesses.

After finishing this book, you'll never be in that situation again.

There are a lot of fallacies about what constitutes a great salesperson. "Oh, he's a great salesperson; he can talk you out of any-thing." "She's a born salesperson." "She has a real sales personality."

As with so many other aspects of life, many people's perceptions of what makes a great salesperson come from Hollywood. Both in the movies and on television, the great salesperson is always a con man type who can talk you out of anything. But how many times can one person talk you out of anything? Only once—and then you'd never buy from that person again. Isn't the great salesperson the one who generates a tremendous amount of repeat business, which leads to bigger sales and more referrals?

Does it take a sales personality, as portrayed on television (outgo-ing, back-slapping, joke-a-minute), to be self-motivated, persistent, and willing to fill customers' needs? No, of course not; that could be anyone. Herb Tarlick, the plaid jacket, white belt, white shoes sales-man of the TV series *WKRP in Cincinnati* was not a good salesper-son. In fact, he was an idiot.

This book will cover the following 16 "rock-solid rules" that successful salespeople follow:

1. They have a great attitude and always do more than they're supposed to do.

2. They see themselves successful.

3. They don't prejudge; they don't assume; they don't minimize themselves, their prospects, or their clients.

4. They are goal oriented. They have written specific goals and strategic plans for their lives, careers, and businesses.

5. The are self-motivated.

6. Successful salespeople are in control.

7. They constantly practice and prepare.

8. They see and talk to more people than anyone else and get more people to say no to them.

9. They take action.

10. They are persistent.

11. They sell more than just the product or service, because they understand who the customer is and what they really want.

12. They consistently create and sell value, rather than get stuck on selling price.

13. They understand that speed and ease are the two biggest benefits you can deliver to a customer.

14. They act as experts, advisers, and resources to their clients, always ready to provide them with knowledge, expertise, information, and education.

15. They are indispensable to their clients.

16. They absolutely, positively love what they do.

As you read this book, you'll find many myths and preconceived notions about selling shattered—and to your benefit, I might add.

You will also notice, as you go through each chapter, that every once in a while I will break away from the topic either to give you a Sales Tip or Sales Alert, or to go off on a Sales Rant, in order to expand on a point and give you more practical information that can be put to use immediately.

This book is no magic formula. You will be asked to do some work in order to come up with your plan. But don't worry, because everything I ask you to do, every idea I give you, will be so easy to implement, you will have no excuse not to do it.

1

Attitude and Commitment: It All Starts Here

Weakness of attitude becomes weakness of character.
— Albert Einstein

ave you ever been walking down the street when you spotted, in the distance, someone who you know is a very depressing person? What do you do? Probably cross the street or duck into the nearest store. Hey, have you ever tried this one? You see him coming so you cover your face, making believe you have to sneeze? Why do you do that? Obviously, because you don't want to talk to that person and end up as depressed as he is.

But, on the other hand, have you ever been walking down the street when you see that very positive and optimistic person coming at you? What do you do then? (By the way, you know you're in big trouble when that person sees you and crosses the street!) I'll bet you make a point of stopping and talking to that person. Why? Naturally, because they make you feel good.

How do you think your clients would react if I posed the same two scenarios to them? Same way, I'll bet! You see, nobody wants to talk to someone who makes them feel lousy, but everyone wants a shot at someone who makes them feel good.

Basic human nature: Everybody wants to associate with a winner. People want to be part of a winning situation and they run like hell from losers. Why do you think winning sports teams sell out most of their games, while losing sports teams can barely give away tickets? Let's face it, if you called the Tampa Bay Devil Rays ticket office and said, "I'm coming to tonight's game and I'm bringing 50 people with me. What time does it start?" their reply would be: "Whenever you get here!"

Most people won't even admit to being part of a losing situation. Did you ever see anyone recommend a bad doctor? What could they possibly say? "Go see this guy, he's a butcher, he'll cut you up but good." On the other hand, have you ever noticed that anytime someone recommends a doctor, they always say, "She's the top person in her field"? Doesn't anyone ever recommend the second or third guy?

As a professional speaker, I think one of the questions I get most often from business owners, executives, and managers is, "It's so hard to find good people, especially good salespeople. What do I look for?" I always say the same thing: Hire attitude. You can teach someone everything they need to know about your company, and in a pretty short period of time, but it's real hard to teach attitude. And let's face it, if they're walking in with a bad attitude before they even have the job, do you really expect it to get better once you're paying them?

I'm not even worried about a person's skills. You know as well as I do that a salesperson with a great attitude but limited skills will do everything in his power to acquire those skills. On the other hand, the salesperson with great skills and a lousy attitude won't use the skills—and if you don't use them, you lose them.

As a salesperson, your attitude and commitment are critical to your success simply because attitude and commitment are what the clients buy. When you speak to a client or prospect your attitude and commitment are what they hear, see, and feel.

Let's face it: No one hears the words. You know as well as I do that most people don't listen; if you have kids, you know that most people don't listen. But people hear your attitude, they feel your commitment, and that's what they're going to buy. Anyone can close a sale, but not everyone can sell attitude and commitment. Only the most successful salespeople can do that.

In my travels, I have met many people who have achieved far more success than was ever expected of them, simply because of their positive attitude and unwavering commitment to do whatever it took to be successful.

Wayne Thorpe's father abandoned his family when Wayne was very young. When he was 13 his mother became quite ill, and he and his three brothers practically raised themselves. Wayne graduated high school an unfocused young man. He started his career cleaning out animal cages for a drug company. But because of his positive attitude, an executive with the company took a liking to him, convinced him he had the ability to do more with his life, and encouraged him to go to college.

Once he saw he was capable of doing more with his life, the confidence he gained fed his burning commitment to succeed. Combining that with his always positive attitude, Wayne Thorpe branched out on his own 15 years ago and now owns and operates a car and limousine service, an auto detailing company, a carpet cleaning company, and a commercial cleaning company. He is one of the most successful entrepreneurs in the city of Durham, North Carolina, and a leader in the minority business community.

His positive attitude has permeated his entire organization and is the number one reason Thorpe's Inc. is so successful. I know this because since 1997 I've been a customer, and in all that time I have never used any other car service to get me to and from the airport. In the last eight years, I have done almost $50,000 worth of business with Thorpe's Inc. just on car trips to and from the airport, and it's all for one reason: the attitude that starts with Wayne Thorpe and permeates his entire organization. And for me it all started with one phone call.

When my wife Linda and I were considering moving from New York City to Chapel Hill, we made numerous trips to research the Chapel Hill area. We checked out everything—schools, neighborhoods, shopping, traffic, cultural activities, airport, and for me, the quality of ground transportation to and from the airport.

One morning, during one of our many research trips, I opened up the local Yellow Pages and found four different car services. I called each one and told them that I would be moving to the area, I was looking for a reliable car service that could get me to and from the airport in Chapel Hill, and I would like to ask them a few questions.

Three of the four acted as if I had the plague and they were afraid they could catch it right through the phone line. Once they knew I wasn't going to spend any money right then and there, they tried to hustle me off the phone as quickly as possible. It was like talking to a New York doctor. (If you've never spoken to a New York doctor, imagine you're speaking to someone who's walking backwards away from you as they're talking to you.)

The fourth company—Thorpe's, of course—spent so much time answering my questions and being helpful, *I* couldn't wait to get *them* off the phone.

The decision was easy—three lousy attitudes, one great one. Eight years and $50,000 worth of business later, I often wonder: If, when I called those other three car services, I had said, "I will be relocating to Chapel Hill, and I'm looking for a reliable car service to take me to and from the airport. I expect to spend approximately $50,000 on this over the next eight years," do you think they would have taken the time to answer my questions?

If every salesperson treated every inquiry as if it were a potential $50,000 client, I'll bet they'd land a lot more $50,000 clients.

My sister-in-law, Brenda Romano, never graduated from college, for one good reason: She never went. After graduating high school, she went to secretarial school. When I first met her, in 1980, she was a secretary at Wrangler Jeans. More than anything she loved music, especially rock music. She loved going to concerts and wanted desperately to get a job in the record business—not an easy thing to do.

Through hard work and hustle, she landed a job as a secretary at RCA records. I would say she worked like a dog, but she would have had to slack off to do that. She always did way more than she was supposed to do. She never let her job description define her.

She stayed late, worked till all hours covering shows performed by RCA's artists, and handled any impossible task with a "No problem" attitude.

Finally she was moved up to the promotion staff and was told that in order to be a promotion person she would have to move to Florida. She did. She did a great job in Florida and was just settling in when she was asked to take over the job in San Francisco, and had to move immediately. From San Francisco to Chicago, from Chicago to New York, from New York to Los Angeles, every time with a "No problem" attitude and everywhere doing a great job by doing more than she was supposed to do.

After moving around to a few different recording labels (always with a better position), she is now president of one of the hottest labels in the industry, Interscope Records, where she is one of the highest ranking women in the entire recording industry. By the way, most of the people who report to her are college graduates.

THE FIRST ROCK-SOLID RULE FOR ACHIEVING SALES SUCCESS
Because of their great attitudes, successful salespeople always do more than they're supposed to do.

Let me stop here for a quick rant regarding rock-solid rule number one.

I'm not a big lover of public schools. I honestly believe most of them are just jobs programs for the marginally employable. One of the many useless lessons kids learn in school is, if you do what you are supposed to do and do that all the time, you'll receive an A or a B. However, in the real world, and especially in the world of sales, doing only what you're supposed to do will get you a C, a nice average grade.

But we're not talking about average here; we're talking about what it takes to be successful. People who work in public schools are government employees. To most government employees, "doing what you're supposed to do" is all that needs to be done. Why do more when you get an annual raise just for hanging around? In sales, if all you do is hang around, you're soon gone.

I received an e-mail not too long ago from one of my radio show listeners that was one of the best examples I've ever seen of someone who succeeded because they were willing to go the extra mile and do more than they were supposed to do. The e-mail came from Deborah Lee, who is a branch manager for a supermarket bank in LaCrosse, Wisconsin. She wrote:

> [While I was] working as a new branch manager for a supermarket bank, a customer came in and after completing his transactions asked if he could borrow a Blue Book for autos. I said, "Sure no problem, If you can please return it on Monday." Well he did, and it was a test. He was out shopping for a new bank to transfer his company's accounts to, and I was the only person that day to give him the time of day, and not question his request.

In case you were wondering, as I was, yes, Deborah landed the account. She didn't do one bit of selling, didn't take even a second to make a presentation. All she did was sell attitude—the attitude that not every customer request is an attempt to put something over on you; the attitude that doing something nice for a customer without any promise of future business does not make you a sap.

The best thing is, Deborah did more than she was supposed to do without really doing anything extraordinary. All Deborah did was grant the customer's request to borrow the Blue Book. Not exactly what I would call going above and beyond the call of duty, but compared to all her competition, she was a regular Mother Teresa.

Do you see how easy it is to beat the competition? In Deborah's case it was loaning out a book with no questions asked. In the case of

Thorpe's Inc. it was the willingness to politely answer a few questions from a potential client. Most salespeople (and most people, for that matter) are so mediocre at what they do that most times, going the extra mile only requires you to go a few extra yards.

In future chapters you'll find that beating the competition is so easy that most times it's just a matter of showing up.

2 | Successful Salespeople See Themselves Successful

Nimble thought can jump both sea and land.

—William Shakespeare

Starting in this chapter, the question I am attempting to answer for you is this: Where do this kind of attitude and commitment come from and what can we do to develop them in our lives and careers? Because, as you'll find as you read on, attitude and commitment are not something we're born with. They must be developed through setting goals, planning, and creating a sense of focus, purpose, and direction for your life and career. You are not born with a burning desire to be the best. There has to be a reason, something you are committed to, and only you can decide what that is.

This chapter also begins my five-step goal-setting and planning process that will help you create your own written five-year plan for your life, career, and business. This plan will give you the sense of purpose, focus, and direction you need to be able to motivate yourself on a consistent basis.

The first step of the goal setting and planning process is to "see it."

THE SECOND ROCK-SOLID RULE FOR ACHIEVING SALES SUCCESS
Successful salespeople see themselves successful. They create visions.

First and foremost, successful salespeople create visions for themselves. They create visions for their lives and careers. And because they're able to create visions for themselves they're also able to create and communicate visions to their clients and prospects. But really, isn't that your job? Isn't that what you're supposed to be doing? Are you just there to get in the door, sell whatever the heck you can, and get out? Or are you there as a resource for that client, someone who will help them create a vision for their company and sell them solutions to their needs?

However, if you cannot even create a vision for yourself, how can you possibly expect to create a vision for someone else? Only if you can *see* yourself successful can you *be* successful. If in your mind you can envision yourself doing something, then you can do it. But if you can't even see yourself doing it in your mind, how can you ever expect to do it in real life?

Have you ever said to yourself, or heard someone else say, "I can't imagine doing that in my wildest dreams"? Well, if you can't do it in your wildest dreams, what makes you think you can do it in real life? Let's face it, it's a lot easier to do this stuff in our dreams.

So see it; see yourself successful; visualize it. What you're trying to do is create a picture in your mind of what you want your success to be.

Now I want you to think of a certain salesperson you probably know. In fact, I'm sure everyone knows someone like this. You've either worked with this person or had someone like this working for you. That salesperson is "the excuse maker."

You know the one I'm talking about—the person who always tells us how much business they could have done, but. . . . They have no luck; they never catch a break. Everyone else is getting the good leads and they're always stuck with the ones that can't pass the credit check. And you know why? "My manager hates me! Everyone here hates me! They're all plotting against me!"

For now, just for the sake of argument, let's say all the excuse makers are right. Even though we know they're wrong, let's say they're right—they have no luck, everyone hates them, and we're all plotting against them. I still have one question for all the excuse makers: How come you still could not even *see* yourself successful? Because nobody stops you from dreaming. And if you don't have good dreams, there's only one thing left: nightmares!

Unfortunately, in this world, there are far more salespeople who fall into the excuse maker category than into the successful salesperson category. Of course, for those of you who are successful or strive to be successful, that's a good thing—it means there's less competition.

In New York City, where I originally come from, we have a saying that goes like this: "Everyone in New York knows someone else who could have bought a building 30 years ago for $9.00."

Have you ever known anyone like this? Better yet, have you ever walked down the street with one of these people? If you have, you'll notice they always say the same thing. The conversation goes like this:

"See that building over there? Thirty years ago I could have bought that building—nine dollars!"

"Well, why dincha?" (Hey, it's New York!)

"Augghh, those lousy jerks, they talked me out of it!"

"Why doncha buy it now?"

"Nahh, it's too late now."

You know what? He's right, it is too late. For him it's too late, and you know why: because he believes it's too late.

We all know people like this. In my travels I've met thousands of these people. I've spoken in front of them. Hell, I've worked with these people.

My first sales job ever started way back in July of 1973. I took a job selling dresses for a dress manufacturer in New York City's garment center. I spent 10 years as a salesman and sales manager in the garment center.

Now I don't know if you know anything about the dress manufacturing business, but in the business there is a saying that goes like this: "You can't do business in December." Every industry has one of these sayings; every company has one of these sayings. I call them the "You-can't-do-business-in" sayings.

In the garment center they say, "You can't do business in December, because the stores are already stocked for Christmas. Nobody's going to buy anything in December to ship in January because January is clearance month and they just want to get rid of inventory. Nobody buys anyone a dress for Christmas; dresses are not a Christmas item." In fact, the saying goes, "It's so bad in December, even the hangers don't fit!"

Well here I was, 21 years old, my first December ever in the garment center. I didn't know you couldn't do business in December—no one ever told me. So, like a dope, every morning I'd get in early, pack my sample bag, and hit the streets. I'd go around to buying offices all morning, and guess what? I was so young, so dumb, so naive—I kept doing business!

But then I heard the voices. They were calling to me, "Hey kid, come here." It was the coffee cup brigade. You know them. The coffee cup brigade are the salespeople who walk around all day holding a coffee cup, telling anyone who'll listen the right way to do things (according to them); what's wrong with the company, the boss, and the product; and how, if they were running things, it would be different. The only problem with the coffee cup brigade is they never do anything, and because of that, they look to drag you down with them.

Well they called me over, and I was dumb enough to listen. They said, "Hey kid, you can't do business in December."

I said, "You can't?"

"Nah, nobody does business in December."

I said, "They don't?"

They said, "Don't even answer the phone, it's only going to be a complaint. Kid, it's so bad in December, even the hangers don't fit."

I said, "Ohmigod!"

But don't worry, by the next December, I knew; I was a veteran. I knew all the things you weren't supposed to know. I knew you couldn't do business in December, and I didn't. Why? Because I listened to all the excuse makers.

And believe me, it doesn't only happen in the garment center.

If average salespeople worked as hard on their job as they did trying to avoid doing their job, their success would be guaranteed. How about these you-can't-do-business-ins: You can't do business in December because everyone's getting ready for the holidays. And you can't do business in January because nobody has any money left over from the holidays. You can't do business in the summer, because everyone's going away on vacation. You can't do business on a Friday because everyone's going away for the weekend, and you certainly can't do business on a Monday—everyone just got back from the weekend and they don't want to pick up the phone.

I'm convinced there's one Wednesday in May that's the only good time of the year to do business.

If you let them, salespeople (and most people, for that matter) will come up with every excuse in the book why it can't be done. Why? Because they have no vision. They don't see themselves successful, they only see themselves failing. In order to fulfill this prophecy they need a reason. So what do they do? They prejudge (most salespeople will call it "qualifying") almost every prospect they come in contact with and decide ahead of time why he or she won't buy.

"Oh, them—I called them three years ago. They're not going to buy from us, our prices are too high." Or how about this: "She had a real bad experience with the last salesperson that had the account. She'll never buy from us again. There's no reason to even call." Or my favorite: "I called him two years ago and he told me he has no need for what we do." Of course, nothing changes over two years. Hell, why bother to call? What could the odds possibly be that the company's needs changed or that that person isn't there anymore? One to one?

It's almost as if these salespeople reject the prospect before the prospect rejects them. I know it happens in your company, because it happens in *every* company!

THE THIRD ROCK-SOLID RULE FOR ACHIEVING SALES SUCCESS
Successful salespeople don't prejudge, don't assume, and don't minimize themselves, their prospects, or their clients.

Now let me tell you a story of a salesperson I know who did not prejudge, did not assume, and did not minimize himself, his prospects, or his clients.

His name is Peter Rosengaard. Peter is a life insurance agent with a company in England named Abbey Life. What makes this story amazing is that back around 1990 Peter got himself into the *Guinness Book of World Records* for sales by selling what was then the single largest life insurance policy on record. Peter sold a life insurance policy with a death benefit of *$100 million* on the life of entertainment entrepreneur David Geffen.

What made it even more amazing was that Peter sold this policy off of a *cold call*.

I met Peter in April 1991. I had just finished delivering a keynote speech to the Life Insurance Association of the United Kingdom in London. After I came off the stage, the members of the organizing committee invited my wife and me out to dinner. They also invited one other guest: Peter. Peter sat next to me at dinner and told me the story of the $100 million sale, and it blew my mind.

It is the perfect example of a salesperson who saw only a prospect with a need. All he saw was someone who needed what he had, and all he could think of was, "They need what I have, they will buy it from someone, so they might as well buy from me."

One day Peter was sitting in his apartment in London reading the newspaper, when he noticed that MCA, the large entertainment company, had just purchased Geffen Records for $600 million.

Peter knew a little about the entertainment industry, having worked in it many years before. He said to himself, "This is a good deal. Geffen Records is a great company." But he also knew something else that he told me: "I knew that while Geffen Records was a good company, David Geffen was the single, indispensable, driving force behind it, and if anything ever happened to David Geffen that $600 million deal would go right down the drain. They needed protection, they needed life insurance."

But now, even if the average salesperson (and unfortunately most salespeople are totally average, doing the same things everyone else does and wondering why they don't work) had thought of this, what do you think the average person says to him- or herself at right about this point? Most likely "Oh I'm sure he already has life insurance." Or "Hey, MCA is a large company. They probably have a dozen guys on the payroll to take care of that stuff." How about, "No way someone like me is going to get in there."

In fact, I asked Peter, "Didn't you even think of that? What were you thinking?"

He answered, "All I could think of was, 'They could have a problem. They have exposure. They need life insurance. Hell, I sell life insurance. They might as well buy it from me.' "

So now Peter decides he's going to cold-call the MCA Corporation. But now, even if the average salesperson gets anywhere near this far, who do you think the average salesperson calls at MCA? Which department do you think they ask for? You'd probably be right if you said human resources or personnel. Hey, don't aim too high, you can fall too far. But you know as well as I do that as a salesperson, if you've ever called personnel or human resources at any large company, they all have the same phone number: 1-800-BRICK WALL!

But not Peter; he decides he's going to cold call the president of MCA, Sid Scheinberg. One afternoon he calls information in the United States. He finds the main switchboard number at MCA, dials the number, and asks for Sid Scheinberg's office. The phone rings and guess what? No, Sid did not answer. Don't try to anticipate me. Actually, Peter got the secretary. He found out that Sid Scheinberg was not in, so he left a message and hung up.

But now, even if the average salesperson got anywhere near this far, what do you think the average salesperson does at this point? You're right if you said they wait for a callback. And if the call doesn't come, what do you think they do? Right again if you answered, "Nothing."

Do you know why? Because the average salesperson is not really concerned with succeeding. The average salesperson is far more concerned with not failing. There is a big difference between succeeding and not failing. And do you know what else the average salesperson is most concerned with? Covering his or her behind. Now they can go to their manager and say, "I tried. I made the call. The guy's not in; this guy is never in. Besides, guys like him don't speak to people like me."

But not Peter. He kept calling and calling and calling, but he could never catch Sid Scheinberg there. But do you know what he did that was not only extremely smart, but extremely easy and cost-effective? He got friendly with the secretary.

 SALES ALERT

Let me take this time to tell you about the secretaries, clerks, and assistants of the world. You see, the secretaries, clerks, and assistants of the world can hardly ever make the decision to say yes. But you better believe they always help make the decision to say no!

And let me tell you something else about the secretaries, clerks, and assistants of the world. Every single decision maker in the world today, at one time or another in his or her career, was a secretary, clerk, or assistant. Now, not every single secretary, clerk, or assistant will grow up one day to be a decision maker, but since none of us are smart enough to know who's going to make it and who is not, it's just a heck of a lot smarter to be nice to every single one.

Peter got real friendly with that secretary at MCA. Then one day he called again. He found out once again that Sid Scheinberg was not there, but this time he learned from the secretary that Sid was in Italy on business. He couldn't find out what hotel he was at, but he got the name of the city. And now the search was on, because what Peter had was a window of opportunity. Let me tell you something about windows of opportunity. They are all around you. They open up for you every day. The problem is they open very quickly, open up just a crack, and then *wham!* They close just as fast.

Peter had his window of opportunity and he jumped right through. So let me back up and give you a little more information about Peter. What you know is that he sells life insurance. What you don't know is how he does it. Peter sells through breakfast appointments. Every day Peter has at least one breakfast appointment with a prospect or a client to sell insurance, and he has these breakfast appointments at the Savoy Hotel in London, which is a 462-star European hotel.

Now I don't know if you know anything about 462-star European hotels, but in 462-star European hotels the concierges all retire as millionaires. You see, they don't get two-dollar tips. They get two-*thousand*-dollar tips.

Peter was having breakfast every day at the Savoy Hotel. Because of this, he struck up a friendship with the concierge and found out from him that all the concierges of all the 462-star hotels in Europe belong to the same club.

One day Peter pulled the concierge from the Savoy aside and asked, "If I was one of the top executives of one of the top entertainment companies in the world, and I was staying in this particular town in Italy, what hotel would I stay at?"

The concierge replied, "Well, there could be only one."

Peter asked, "Would you happen to know the concierge at that hotel?"

The concierge said, "Of course, we belong to the same club."

"Could you call and find out if Sid Scheinberg is staying there?" asked Peter, and of course the concierge said yes.

So the concierge in London called the concierge in Italy and found out that, yes indeed, Sid Scheinberg was at that hotel. Whoa, window of opportunity!

Now Peter had to make the call. But you know as well as I do, you don't just make a call. You have to plan it out. You have to know what you're going to say ahead of time, because you only get one shot at a first impression.

Peter thought about it and told me, "I had to know what I was going to say, but I also had to know the perfect time to call. I know when these big shots come to Europe they always dress for dinner. Dinner is around 7:30, cocktails about 6:30. I figured if I called his room at 5:30 in the afternoon, not only would I catch him in, but I just might catch him standing there in his underwear!"

At 5:30 in the afternoon Peter called the hotel in Italy. When the switchboard answered he said, "Sid Scheinberg's room, please." The phone rang and this time Sid answered, "Sid Scheinberg here."

But now, even, *even* if the average salesperson gets anywhere near this far, what do you think the average salesperson says? Yeah, you got it: "Homina, homina, homina." Why? Because average salespeople never believe that this kind of stuff could ever happen to them. You see, they have no vision; they don't see themselves successful, they only see themselves failing.

But not Peter. Very calmly and quickly he said, "Mr. Scheinberg, Peter Rosengaard here from Abbey Life in London. Mr. Scheinberg, congratulations on that shrewd deal of buying Geffen Records for $600 million."

I thought that was a pretty smart thing to say, wouldn't you agree? Don't you think he wanted to be told he did something good? Doesn't everybody? Don't you? Besides, what do you think the media was probably saying about the deal when it was first done? Probably what they always say: "Paid too much." Then five years later what do they usually say? "Boy, was he lucky to get that so cheap." This is why the people who write the articles never seem to be as successful as the ones who make the deals.

Well, Peter congratulated Sid Scheinberg, and Sid thanked him. But let's not forget, Sid Scheinberg did not become successful because he had just fallen off the turnip truck. He knew something was up and said, "Thank you. What do you want?"

Peter said, "Mr. Scheinberg, while buying Geffen Records for $600 million was a really shrewd deal, you know as well as I do that David Geffen is the single, most indispensable force behind Geffen Records. Did you ever think of what might happen to your $600 million investment should something happen to David Geffen?"

What do you think one of the biggest executives at one of the biggest entertainment companies in the world said? He said, "Gee, we never thought of that. What did you have in mind?" Whoa, *window of opportunity!*

But now, even, *even* if the average salesperson got anywhere *near* this far, what kind of number do you think the average person throws out? Probably $1 million; that always seems to be the number for the average salesperson.

However, I want you to remember something: You are speaking to a man who has just written a check for *$600 million!* A million dollars to this guy is a *tip!* But average salespeople have a huge fear of large numbers. Why? Because they never truly believe those kind of numbers could ever be a part of their lives. They have no vision; they never see themselves successful; they only see themselves failing.

But not Peter. Very calmly and quickly he replied, "I thought $100 million would be a great place to start." And the man who had written a check for $600 million said, "Sounds reasonable to me. Let's get it done." Sometimes it can be that easy, if you give it a shot and keep trying.

Sid said to Peter, "Here's my assistant's number. You call him and tell him what you told me and let's get this done."

Months later, after all the paperwork, underwriting, and medical exams, and after they ran it past the sales prevention department (I'll bet you know those folks, too), Peter Rosengaard closed the deal for the $100 million life insurance policy and got himself into the *Guinness Book of World Records*.

All this happened because he never prejudged, never assumed, never minimized himself or his prospect. All he saw was a prospect with a need. All he saw was someone who needed what he had, and his only attitude was, "They need what I have. They will buy it from someone. They might as well buy it from me."

One other thing Peter did, or rather didn't do: Not *once* throughout the entire process did Peter Rosengaard ever stop seeing himself successful.

So see it; see yourself successful. Create in your mind a picture of what you want your success to be. Once you've created that picture of success in your mind, focus—focus in so clearly on that picture that you can describe it right down to its most minute details. Once you can focus on and describe clearly what it is you want, you're ready for the next step.

3

Setting Goals: Why You Need Them and Why You Need to Write Them Down

A successful life is one that is lived through understanding and pursuing one's own path, not chasing after the dreams of others.

—Chin-Ning Chu

THE FOURTH ROCK-SOLID RULE FOR ACHIEVING SALES SUCCESS
Successful salespeople are goal oriented. They have written specific goals and plans for their lives, careers, and businesses.

True motivation is an internal force. It has to come from within. Nobody else can motivate you. Sure, I'm known as a motivational speaker and I can get up in front of a group, deliver a fire-and-brimstone speech, and have the audience swinging from the chandeliers. But 24 hours later they're going to wake up and say, "Who was that guy?"

What I try to do in my talks and what I'm attempting to do in this book is to give you the tools and techniques that will better enable you to motivate yourself.

Most salespeople are not self-motivated (as is the case with most people). They have no idea what motivates them. They have no goals and no plan for their lives, careers, or businesses. Let's face it, if you don't know what you want, what's the motivation to go out and get it?

So often I sit in an audience, waiting to get up on stage to speak, and I'll listen to a CEO tell hundreds of people, "If we work real hard this year and put our noses to the grindstone, this company will do great!" I'll look out into that audience and see all those people saying to themselves, "Who cares—what's in it for me?"

Now here's the tricky part of the deal. If you were to go out into that audience and ask all those people, "What do you want to be in it for you?" I guarantee most of them couldn't tell you. How do you motivate people like that? The only way I know is to help them figure out what it is they want, and then show them how to use their job or career as a vehicle for getting it. In this way, these same people are now working for themselves, and when you're working for yourself and constantly moving toward the rewards you want, the motivation will just pour right out of you.

THE FIFTH ROCK-SOLID RULE FOR ACHIEVING SALES SUCCESS
Successful salespeople are self-motivated.

What makes successful salespeople self-motivated? Simple—they have a clearly defined focus, direction, and sense of purpose for their lives, careers, and businesses. They know exactly what it is they want to achieve and when they will achieve it by, and they have clearly defined the specific steps they will take to achieve these goals.

This focus, direction, and sense of purpose keep successful salespeople on track and motivated. They know every morning when they wake exactly where they're going and how they're going to get there. Because they are so focused, it's hard, let's say almost impossible, for other people to come along and get them off track.

It's easy to knock the average salesperson off track. They'll go in any direction they're asked to, since they don't have one of their own.

As you can see, it all starts with a sense of purpose or a goal, and that goal must be written down.

Now before you start to say, "What hope do I have? I hate my job, I hate my boss, I can't seem to get motivated, and I'm certainly not ever going to do enough business to be successful," remember, this is not brain surgery. If it was I wouldn't be doing it.

Every time I meet a top producing salesperson I ask the same question: "Tell me how you got to where you are, and what happened when you first started." You know what the vast majority say? "I was a total failure when I first started. Only when I sat down and mapped a plan for myself that I stuck to, did I move in the right direction." I have yet to meet a successful salesperson (or any successful person) who didn't have clearly defined written goals and a plan.

So there's hope for everyone and anyone. In fact, the reason I am so adamant, to the point of being fanatical, about having written goals and plans is because goal setting has been responsible for the success of every major change in my life, and it will continue to get me everything I want for the future.

I was one of those unmotivated, directionless people walking around in a comatose state, mumbling, "I hate my job; I don't want to do this anymore. But what else could I possibly do? This is the only thing I know. And besides, they pay me well, so I might as well stay." Whoa, talk about commitment! "They pay me well, so I might as well stay." How would you like to have someone like that working for you?

It was 1983. I had spent almost 10 years working in the garment center in New York City and I *hated* it! But instead of constantly whining that I was stuck and "what else could I do," I had a revelation. I said to myself, "Hey, putz, it's not that there's nothing else you can do—there's always something else you can do. It's just that you're too lazy to get off your big fat ass to figure out what it is."

So that's what I did. I got off my big fat ass (it's much smaller now), went to see a career counselor, was put through my first ever goal setting session, and within months had the career I wanted along with a job that I created! I was head of sales and marketing for a small training and consulting firm in New York City.

After two years on that job I decided I wanted to be in my own business. I went back to my goal setting skills (which were now even sharper, since I went to every goal setting and training seminar that I sold) to write a plan for my new business. I started my business in March 1986 and I'm still out there going strong.

Probably the biggest change I ever made was in 1997 when my wife, children, and I relocated from New York City (where we had lived our entire lives) to Chapel Hill, North Carolina. Every time I tell people that, they always say the same thing: "Wow, that's a big change!" I know, that's why we did it. If I wanted a small change, I would have moved to the east side.

But, as with any other big change in my life, I didn't just wake up one day and say to my wife, "We gotta get the hell out of here, so let's throw a dart into the map of the United States and wherever it hits, that's where we go."

We started discussing this three years before we left, and after asking the inevitable question, "Where do we go?" we took our goal setting and planning skills and formulated criteria and a profile of what we felt would be the perfect place for our family.

After narrowing it down and coming up with Chapel Hill, we then visited it so many times we knew every inch of the place. It was only then that we knew it would be the perfect place for us, and it has been.

Having a clearly defined written goal and plan will motivate and energize you to go out and achieve anything you really want in your life, career, or business. I'm always amazed at how easy it's been for me to get whatever I want, once I bother to figure out what it is.

Now that I've told why you need goals, let me give you three specific reasons why you need to write them down:

1. *So you don't forget.* Now I know this sounds pretty stupid, but did you ever wake up in the middle of the night with a good idea—the kind of idea that's so good, it wakes you out of a sound sleep at 3 A.M., the kind of idea that you know is going to make you millions of dollars? What did you do? Most people say, "I went back to sleep." If you did, what happened to the great idea when you woke up the next morning? Gone! How about those people who wrote it down? They usually say they woke up, looked at

the paper, got real excited about the great idea, and started working toward it.

Bingo! Things that sound dumb, but are true: One of the three most important reasons you need to write down your goals is so you don't forget. I know what you're going to say: "Hey, my goals are important to me. These are the things I want most in my life. I'm not going to forget them. I don't need to write them down." Yeah, right. That idea that woke you up at 3 A.M. was pretty important, too. It was going to make you millions. You didn't write that one down, and four hours later, at 7 A.M., it was gone. How long till you forget your goals—eight hours? Sixteen? Twenty-four?

2. *The writing down of a goal is the first commitment to actually going out and accomplishing it.* I really believe we all have goals, we all have dreams. But you know the big stuff you want? I mean the *really* big stuff. You know as well as I do that those are the kind of goals that could take you 2, 3, 5, 10 years of time, energy, and effort to achieve. Let me ask you this: If you're not willing to take 5 or 10 minutes to write it down, what makes you think you'll be willing to invest 5 or 10 years of time, energy, and effort toward achieving it? It's a lot easier to write it down than to go out and get it. If you're not willing to do the easy, what makes you think you'll ever be willing to do the hard?

3. *The writing down of a goal makes you accountable to the only person you can't fool: you.* Admit it; you can fool anyone you want. You can fool your spouse, parents, kids, boss, co-workers, friends, and every living relative, but there's one person who always knows the God's-honest truth: you. How are you going to feel when you have to admit to yourself that you weren't willing to do everything it takes to achieve what you said you wanted? As a matter of fact, I have actually met

people who didn't want to write down their goals because then they wouldn't have to take accountability. Pretty shrewd, huh? (That's sarcasm, folks.) All I know is no matter how much you try to run and hide, you still have to look in the mirror every day.

Okay, I've told you why. In the next chapter I'm going to *show* you why. And I'm going to show you why in a way that is so easy for you to relate to and so much a part of your everyday life that there will be no way for you to dispute me—and no chance for you to come up with an excuse about why you can't do it.

4

Successful Salespeople Are in Control

You cannot prevent the birds of sorrow from flying over your head, but you can prevent them from building nests in your hair.

—Chinese Proverb

In Chapter 3, I told you why you need to write down your goals. But now, as promised, I'm going to *show* you why, and I'm going to start by asking you a question.

Have you ever done the grocery shopping at home? I mean real grocery shopping—not you single guys out there whose refrigerator contains a jar of mayonnaise and a six-pack. Funny thing is, I know why the six-pack is there, but why the mayonnaise?

Ask any single guy and they always say the same thing: "For sandwiches." But they never have any bread or meat. It's almost as if they live in hope that someone will come along one day with bread and meat, before the mayonnaise turns green.

However, for those who do real food shopping, have you ever used a written shopping list? Now if you answered yes, have you also gone shopping without a written list? What's the difference?

Most people say they buy more, spend more time and money, and forget things when they don't have a written shopping list. So what they're actually saying is that when they go out there without a written, focused direction and plan, they end up wasting time, wasting money, taking on a lot of things they did not need, and forgetting a lot of things they did. Oh, by the way, did I mention anything about food shopping in that last sentence? No, I didn't, and I'll bet that could apply to your life.

Did you ever notice when you go grocery shopping with a list how the shopping just seems to flow? You go aisle by aisle and before you know it, you're done. In fact, can you make up a shopping list by aisle? Don't laugh, a lot of people can, and you know what? Their shopping gets done faster than everyone else's. And you know why? Because they see themselves successful. In other words, they've visualized it. By writing up that shopping list by aisle, they actually do the shopping in their mind before they ever get to the store.

But have you ever noticed when you go without a list, you always seem to be running from one end of the store to the other. You grab something off a shelf, and then you realize you forgot something that's down at the other end. You run over there, grab it, realize you forgot something else, and have to run all the way back. You can't say, "I'll get it later," because you're afraid if you don't do it now, you'll forget (since, of course, you didn't write it down).

Has this ever happened to you: Did you ever have a conversation with the peanut butter shelf? You know what I mean—you stand in front of the peanut butter and say, "Do we have that? I'm sure we ran out. No, no, I think there are a couple of jars in the cabinet. No, I'm sure the kids told me we ran out." Meanwhile, people are walking past wondering, "Why is this crazy person talking to the peanut butter shelf?" Finally, you grab a jar off the shelf and say, "Oh what the hell, I'll buy a jar!" Then you get home and what do you find? Three jars of peanut butter, from the other three conversations you had with the peanut butter shelf.

Let's take it a step further. In surveys of the many audiences I've spoken to, this is what they said happens when they go food shopping with and without a list. With a list:

- It takes about 10 minutes to write the shopping list.
- It takes about 1.5 hours to do the shopping (including round-trip travel and bagging, loading, and unloading the groceries).

Now look what happens without the list. Without a list:

- They waste an additional 30 minutes shopping.
- They spend about $40 to $50 extra.

Remember, these numbers are not mine. These are responses of people in my audience. People just like you.

What these numbers show us is that the willingness to stop, sit down, and take 10 minutes up front to develop a written, focused direction and plan in something as unimportant and irrelevant as grocery shopping (if I asked you to name the top 10 priorities in your life, I doubt that grocery shopping would make the list—at least I hope not) yielded these results within only an hour and a half (the time it takes to shop with a list):

- Within 1.5 hours a 30-minute savings, or a 75 percent return on their investment in time.

- $40 to $50 extra in their pocket.

Let's stop here for one of my rants:

This is what planning is: a willingness to stop running off in a million different directions that lead to nowhere, in order to create a focused direction that will lead us to what we really want.

There are too many people who believe that if they're not running around like lunatics, giving the appearance of being busy, then they're not accomplishing anything. If you ever run into these people, they always look frazzled and stressed out. Try to talk to them and they'll say, "Can't talk now, gotta run, gotta do, too much on my plate."

They're the kind of people who buy appointment calendars and date books that are so complicated you have to take a seminar to learn how to use them. These people can't make an appointment to see you because they don't know how to use their own book.

Do you know what I call these people? Human gerbils. You know what a gerbil is—it's a hamsterlike, ratty type animal. It lives in a cage and it plays on a wheel. If you know anything about gerbils, you know they are the busiest little suckers in the world! They get on that wheel and they just fly. And when they're done, they just lie there exhausted, because they're *so damn busy!*

But notice something about gerbils: They never get anywhere; they never get off the wheel. That's what happens to people who aren't willing to stop and take a step back in order to take three steps forward.

So, to repeat, the willingness to stop, take a step back, sit down and take 10 minutes to create a written, focused direction and plan in something as unimportant and irrelevant to your life as food shopping, within only 1.5 hours (talk about instant gratification) got you back 30 minutes (a 75 percent return on investment in time) and put an extra $40 to $50 in your pocket.

Can you imagine what kind of return on your investment you could get if you did something like this for your life, career, or business? *That's why you write down your goals!*

Here's an exercise for you to do, using the following time line. As you notice, on the left-hand side of the line is the year 2001. On the right hand side is 2006. What I want you to do is to plug in along this line, according to the year it happened, the most significant things that have happened to you in the past five years.

It's whatever you consider significant, good or bad (since no one else has to look at this, you can even put down the disgusting stuff). Take only about one minute and just write down the first things that come to your mind. If you have a year where nothing significant happened, don't worry about it.

If you really have to think about it, believe me, it wasn't too significant.

2001_____

   2002_____

      2003_____

         2004_____

            2005_____

                  2006

All right, that's more than enough time. Again, if you're still thinking, it wasn't the least bit significant. Now I want you to go back over those items you listed and draw a circle around any item that you had either direct or indirect control over. By the way, I once had a member of my audience say to me, "My wife gave birth last year, should I circle that?" I said, "How the hell am I supposed to know?"

What did you find when you drew your circles? I'll tell you what the vast majority of people find: They find that they have circled all of them, and those that didn't have circled all of the items except maybe one.

What does that tell you? Right! You're in control—or, as my 14-year-old daughter would say, "Duh!"

You control your life and you control your destiny. Whether you believe it or not, and whether you want to believe it or not, it doesn't matter, because it's true anyhow. We all control the things that happen to us in our lives. In fact, I'll bet if you were really honest about the items you didn't circle, you would admit that maybe you really did have direct or indirect control over them.

Here's something you might want to do. Make a copy of that time line along with all your circled entries on a piece of paper. Take that piece of paper, fold it up, put it in your pocket, and always carry it around with you. The next time you get into one of those situations where you believe you have no control, take out that piece of paper and look at all the circles.

Of course, many salespeople don't like to admit they are in control, because they would have to be accountable. It's a lot easier to blame it on luck, bad breaks, the credit department, the stupid prospect, or the competition who undercut you on price. Which brings me to rule number six.

THE SIXTH ROCK-SOLID RULE FOR ACHIEVING SALES SUCCESS
Successful salespeople are in control. They control their lives, their careers, and their destinies.

One of the things I've noticed about successful salespeople is they are not afraid to take the heat when something goes wrong. If they lose a sale they're going to find out why and fix it. Conversely, when they close a particularly tough sale, they're going to remember how they did it and try to duplicate it the next time they get into a similar situation.

It is their attention to detail and willingness to take that step back in order to plan ahead that keeps them in control of their lives, businesses, and destinies.

As you'll learn in the next couple of chapters, successful salespeople are never without a goal or plan for everything they do or want to accomplish. Whether it's a sales plan, activity plan, a plan of attack for landing a new client, a marketing plan, a script for planning out phone calls and objections, or the master plan for their lives and careers, successful salespeople's ability to anticipate situations and plan ahead for them is one of the many things that differentiates them from their competition.

Now that you understand how you control your life and destiny, I want you to do something.

Look at the next time line. Notice that now the year 2006 is on the left side, and on the right side we have 2011. Now that you understand that you control your life and destiny, what I want you to do is plug in along this line the most significant things that you would *like* to see happen to you in the next five years!

2006_____2011

But wait, not so fast. Now we have rules and criteria, because this is far more important than the last exercise. The last exercise was about stuff that had already happened—it's done, over with. This exercise is about things that have yet to happen, and this is now even more exciting, since we now know how much control we have over these future events—if we plan them properly. To find out what these rules are, turn to the next chapter.

5

The Three Components of an Effective Written Goal

The major reason for setting a goal is for what it makes of you to accomplish it. What it makes of you will always be the far greater value than what you get.

—Jim Rohn

Before you begin to make your list of the most significant things you would like to see happen to you in the next five years, there are three rules I want you to follow. They are the three components of an effective written goal.

Please Be Specific

Please do not write down, "Next year I want to make more money," or, "I'd like to get a better job," "Live in a nicer house," and so on. One question: What the hell does that mean?! What is "more money"? If I gave you a nickel you'd have more than you started out with, but I don't think that's what you're looking for. How do you define what a better job is? And if you can't, how can you possibly expect to find it?

Most people have vague goals. They talk in code words: a lot, more, better, nicer. Let me ask you, what's a lot of money? Could be anything, because what's a lot to one person is not necessarily a lot to another person. And the thing about "a lot" is, it doesn't matter what your "a lot" is; what matters is that *you know* what it is. Because only if you know what it is and can define it can you formulate a plan to get it.

Almost 20 years ago, when I was first starting out in my business as a professional speaker, I was conducting a seminar in New York City. I asked the audience to give me their definition of success. Of course I got what I call "the usual suspects." They said things like money, power, fame, recognition.

I turned to the young man who said "Money," and asked, "What do you mean by money? Do you mean a lot of money?" He said, "Yes, a lot of money."

I asked him, "What's a lot of money?"

He said, "Whatever will make me comfortable."

I said, "What will make you comfortable?"

He said, "Whatever will give me everything I want."

I said, "What do you want?"

He said, "A lot of money."

Well, we went around in this circle for what seemed like hours, till I finally said, "Hey pal, give me a number. What's a lot?" He said, "Eighty billion dollars." Now I had to admit, that's a lot! But I want you to see what happened next.

I said to him, "Okay, you got it. I'm going to give you $80 billion. What are you going to do with it?" You see, if you don't know what you're going to do with it, what's the motivation to get it?

 SALES ALERT

Here's another question for you: How many sales do you have to close to make a lot of money? That's right: a lot! But now, how many prospects do you have to see to get to close a lot of sales to make a lot of money? A lot more than that! But hold it: How many calls do you have to make to get to see a lot of people to close a lot of sales to make a lot of money? *One hell of a lot!*

How do you know when to stop? And don't say you don't stop, because you stop every day. In fact, if you're reading this book right now, you're stopped. If you don't know what your "a lot" is, how do you know you didn't stop short? Do you ever have one of those days when the first three people you call say, "Drop dead"? What do you do? You probably slam down the phone and say, "Okay, that's a lot!" How do you know you didn't have to speak to five people that day, because you don't know what your "a lot" is?

Uh-oh, I feel another rant coming on.

Why do you think so many lottery winners go broke? They never thought, for a moment, what they would do with the money if they ever got it, so they just blow it.

Have you ever seen TV interviews with people lined up to buy lottery tickets when there's a big jackpot that week? I love when they ask, "What would do if you won?" My favorite answers:

- "I would pay off my debt."
- "I'd buy my mother a house."
- "I'd travel around the world."

Does he really need to win the lottery to pay off his debt? What kind of debt could this idiot possibly have? How would you like to be one of the suckers that loaned this guy money? The only way you're going to get your money back is if he wins the lottery! I have a good piece of advice for you: Don't start making plans to spend this big windfall.

Do people really need to win the lottery to buy a house or travel around the world? And what are these people really saying? Are they saying they have pinned all their greatest hopes and dreams on winning the lottery, which is something like a 10 million to 1 shot? When they don't win (and most likely they won't), does that mean they're going to give up all their hopes and dreams?

By doing something you love, working hard at it, and saving your money, you have better than a 1 in 100 chance of being a millionaire. But when you have no goals, don't know where you're going or how you're going to get there, buying a lottery ticket sure seems like the best way out.

No goals, no plan equals a 10 million to 1 shot. Taking a little bit of time to develop a written, focused direction, goal, and sense of purpose can give you a 100 to 1 shot. The choice is up to you.

Let's go back to the young man who wanted "a lot" of money and finally said $80 billion was a lot. When I asked what he was going to do with it he said, "I'm going to spend it." He must have thought he was a senator. So I asked, "What are you going to spend it on?" and he said, "I'm going to buy everything."

Now I'm trying to visualize how someone actually does that, and I said, "What are you going to do, back up a truck to Macy's and buy everything?" He said, "No, you don't understand (you're damn straight I didn't), I'm going to buy the United States."

I said "Stop! Stop right there. Could you buy the United States for $80 billion?" He said No. I replied, "Well, then is that a lot of money?" He said, "I guess not."

You see, it's only a lot if it gets you what you want. But if you don't know what you want, how do you know what you have to do to get it? And, if you don't know what it is, how do you know you didn't already have it, but because you couldn't recognize it at the time, you just let it pass you by? People pass up some of the greatest opportunities in their lives, because they never bother to figure out what kind of opportunities they're looking for.

Let's get this out of the way right up front: Money is not a motivator. Nobody ever wakes up in the morning and says, "I can't wait to get to work today, because they pay me well." Money is not something that makes people love their jobs; it's only something that might allow you not to hate it so much.

Money is a vehicle. It is a vehicle that allows you to live the type of lifestyle you choose to live. Therefore, what we really need to know is what type of lifestyle we want. If you can answer the question, "How do I want my life to look?" then you'll be able to figure out how much money you need to support that lifestyle. That amount of money becomes your "a lot," and now you can formulate a sales plan to earn that amount of money. That's being specific.

Use Time Frames

When you write down each item you want to accomplish in the next five years, also write down the year you intend to accomplish it by. Remember, a goal is a dream with a deadline.

By giving ourselves deadlines, we're making sure we get up off our rear ends and get going. If you leave the time frame open-ended, what's the motivation to start?

Too many salespeople, even if they have specific goals, have vague time frames. They talk about getting things done "eventually" or "sometime." I had a friend like that. He was always threatening to start his own business. I say "threatening," rather than "promising," because the way he went about it, it was more of a threat than a promise.

He was like Kramer in the TV show *Seinfeld*. He always had great ideas and was always way ahead of his time. But every time I asked him when he was going to implement one of those ideas and get the business rolling, he would always say, "I'm researching it and I'll get around to it sometime."

He spent so much time researching, he would have been better off opening a research library, because he never got any of those great ideas off the ground. Invariably, a couple of years later he would see one of those ideas that someone else acted on and he'd say, "See, that was my idea." So what?

It's a funny thing, this word *sometime*. It has the word *time* in it, but the way we use it, it really means "never." So let's explore this word *sometime*.

What if you targeted me as one of your prospects, called me on the phone to set up an appointment, and said, "Warren, can I come over and see you sometime?" and I said, "Yes," and hung up. When would you come over? It better be right away, because other than that, you have no idea when I'm going to be there.

How about this: Have you ever asked one of your kids to do

something, whether it is a household chore or, most likely their homework? I'll bet you had to ask over and over again when it would get done. And when you do ask, what do they usually say? "Don't worry, I'll get around to it sometime." What does that answer tell you? It tells you you're nowhere near finished nagging them to do it.

Here's a good one: You're walking down the street and you see this person coming at you. It's someone you know and while it's not someone you dislike, it is someone who, if you never saw them again, it would be no big deal. But they spotted you before you could cross the street or duck into a store, and now you're stuck speaking with this person. It usually goes something like this:

You: "Hey, how ya doing?" (Okay, so this conversation is taking place in Brooklyn.) "Haven't seen you in years, you look great. Did you lose weight? Why don't you give me a call and we could get together *sometime*. Better yet, give me your number and I'll call you *sometime*."

Why do you say that? Because you have no desire to ever see that person again. We use that word *sometime* when we don't want to do or have no intention of doing something. So what are we saying when we stick that word *sometime* on the end of our goals, dreams, and aspirations?

When you write down what it is that you want, write down the year you intend to achieve it by.

Place No Limits on Your Ability to Achieve

I am now going to tell you something you have probably never heard before: I do not believe in setting realistic goals. I think "realistic" or "reasonable" goals are crap. If it's what you really want, write it down.

When people say, "Set realistic goals," they are using the word *re-*

alistic as a code word. What it really means is "low." In other words, set your goals low enough so that there is no way you can fail. Hey, what are we trying to do here, succeed or "not fail"?

Of course, every time I say I hate realistic goals, I always get someone challenging me. A couple of years ago, a young salesman approached right after one of my talks and said, "You said you don't believe in realistic goals. Okay, next year I want to make $10 million!"

I said, "So, who's stopping you? Do you really think no one in this country has ever made ten million dollars in a year? It's been done plenty of times."

Then I proceeded to tell that young salesman exactly what he would have to do to earn that $10 million, and he said, "Whoa, that's not *realistic*." Gotcha! It's not the goal that wasn't realistic, it's that he wasn't willing to do what it takes to achieve the goal—maybe because, more than anything, it wasn't what he really wanted.

You'll find, when we get to the next chapter on developing your action plan, the questions that determines whether a goal is realistic is, when you sit down to formulate your plan, are you willing to do what it takes to achieve the goal? If you are, then any goal is realistic. If you're not, then even the simplest goal becomes difficult.

Besides, what's realistic? Most people believe anything that's never been done before is unrealistic. Thank God, not everyone thinks that way or there'd be no innovation in the world. I'll never forget, in early 1969, Alvin Dark, who managed several major league baseball teams, including the A's and Giants, was asked when he thought the Mets (who had been perennial losers through their entire seven-year existence) might ever win a World Series. He said, "When a man lands on the moon."

Now I don't know how good your memory is, but in the summer of 1969, Neil Armstrong became the first man to land on the moon, and in October 1969, the New York Mets won the World Series—two occurrences that were considered "unrealistic" less than a year before.

Too many people also believe that anything that seems hard or out of the ordinary is not realistic. In September 1972, four months after graduating from college, I put a pack on my back and headed off to Europe, where I traveled around for the next four months. One of the many things I'll never forget about that experience is the reaction of so many people to my plans. They said, "You're so smart to do this now, because when you get older, you'll never have this chance again."

That was one of the two most frightening things I ever heard in my life. The other was when my former boss in the garment center thought he was doing me a favor when he said to me, "Don't worry, you'll have a job here for the rest of your life." Both statements felt like prison sentences.

I thought to myself, "Do people really believe your life is over at the age of 21?" I refused to believe I'd never have the chance to do that again. Is being able to travel through Europe past the age of 21 unrealistic?

The average person can't think beyond his own self-imposed limitations. The message was constantly pounded into us: Grow up, go to school, graduate from college, get a job, get married, have a family, take your two weeks vacation, and when you're 65, you can enjoy yourself—if you don't drop dead of conformity first.

Luckily for me, I always questioned this thinking. However, it wasn't until 11 years later, when I learned about the power of goal setting, that the possibilities started to become limitless. Now, as a professional speaker, I get to travel all over the world, get paid for doing it, and the best part is I don't have to schlep a backpack or sleep in youth hostels (or worse).

As a successful salesperson you, too, have limitless possibilities. There is no goal that is unrealistic. If we look at a career breakdown of millionaires, you'll find there are far more millionaires from the ranks of salespeople than doctors or attorneys.

Again, what's realistic? If a young girl, nine years old, said to you, "When I get older, I'm going to be an Olympic gymnast," would you tell her, "That's not realistic"? I hope not. It's hard, but it's not unrealistic. Let's not confuse hard with unrealistic. Someone is going to make that Olympic gymnastics squad—why not that nine-year old girl?

Instead of someone telling her the goal is unrealistic, she'd be better off if someone told her all that it's going to take, especially the hard work, sacrifice, and commitment that are necessary to even have a shot of qualifying for the Olympics.

In sales, one of the biggest roadblocks you'll face toward achieving success will come from your colleagues and co-workers. Other people are always so ready, willing, and able to tell us why our goals, dreams, and aspirations can't be accomplished. And they're right— *they* can't do it. But neither can you if you listen to them.

The biggest reason other people will try to stop you is because they don't want you to be more successful than they are. For them, it's easier to hold you back than it is to work harder to keep up with you. It's the old "Don't work too hard, you're making us look bad" mentality.

Many of my clients ask me to speak at their "Top Producers Conference." These are incentive conferences for the top 5 to 20 percent of a company's salespeople. There are two things I've always noticed about top producers conferences:

1. Even though the rules for qualifying are the same for every salesperson in the organization, the same people seem to qualify year after year after year.
2. They always seem to be held in the small room.

If you recall, in the Introduction to this book I stated that if we looked at every sales organization in the world, we'd find, for the most part, they break down the same way. Ten percent of the salespeople are great; 10 percent should be kicked down the stairs and out the door; and the other 80 percent are totally average.

If you are one of the 10 percent at the top, fantastic: keep doing what you're doing and never stop going after those unrealistic goals. If you are one of the 80 percent in the middle who really wants to get into the top 10 percent, see the next Sales Alert.

 SALES ALERT

The best and easiest way to start moving toward the top 10 percent is to stop hanging around with the bottom 10 percent and spend more time interacting with the top 10 percent.

Unfortunately, this is not as easy as I'm making it sound. There are two very good reasons why the salespeople in the middle 80 percent spend far more time with the 10 percent at the bottom than with the 10 percent at the top.

1. The 10 percent at the top are never around. *They're busy!* That's why they're the 10 percent at the top!

2. The bottom 10 percent are *always* around. They have nothing better to do. That's why they're the bottom 10 percent.

What makes it even worse is these bottom 10 percenters are the proverbial rotten apple that spoils the whole barrel. They would rather bring you down to them than put in the time, energy, and effort to rise up to you. In sales offices all over the world, here's the kind of wisdom being generated by the bottom 10 percent in conversations with the middle 80 percent:

Bottom: "Hey, why are you working so hard? You don't want to do that. Let's get some coffee."

Bottom: "Hey, you like working here."

Middle: "Yeah, I do."

Bottom: "You must be nuts. First chance I get, I'm outta here." (Sure, like everyone is lined up waiting to hire this clown.)

Bottom: "Hey, what do think of _____ (manager's name)?"

Middle: "I like him/her."

Bottom: "Are you kidding? He's a moron. I don't know how he got the job. Must have had dirty pictures on the boss."

By the way, these conversations, more than lack of production, are the number one reason why managers should just fire bottom 10 percenters. As Casey Stengel, the Hall of Fame manager of the Yankees, once said when asked the key to being a great manager, "On any ball club, one third of your players hate you, one third love you, and the other third are on the fence. The key to being a great manager is to make sure you keep the one third on the fence away from the one third who hate you."

You will learn more about being a successful salesperson in five minutes with a top 10 percenter than you could in five *years* with a bottom 10 percenter. Approach one of the top producers in your office and offer to take him to lunch. Tell him you want to be more successful and you'd love to pick his brain to find out what he did to get from where you are now to where he is.

So think about it: What's realistic? If some young girl had approached you 30 years ago and said, "Someday I'm going to be one of the most famous entertainers in the world, and I'm going to do it by wearing my underwear outside my clothes," you would have thought that was not only unrealistic but insane. However, that young girl became Madonna, and one of the things Madonna did to become famous and separate herself from her competition was to wear her underwear on the outside. In fact, she started a fashion trend.

1. Be specific.

2. Use time frames.

3. Place no limits on your ability to achieve; if it's what you really want, write it down.

These are the three components of an effective written goal.

Now that you know this, go back to the last page of Chapter 4 and plug in along that line the most significant things that you would like to see happen to you in the next five years.

As you're writing down these goals, visualize them; see yourself successful. If you can see the goal in your mind, it will make it that much easier to be specific. Take some time and do it now.

6

The Action Plan: Why You Need One

Whatever failures I have known, whatever errors I have committed, whatever follies I have witnessed in private and public life have been the consequence of action without thought.

—Bernard Baruch, stockbroker, adviser to presidents
Woodrow Wilson and Harry S. Truman (1870–1965)

Now that you have written down the most significant things you would like to see happen to you in the next five years, I want you to understand what you have just done. You have started the process. You have set some goals. You have created destinations for yourself that state, "This is what I want to accomplish over the next one to five years, and this is when I intend to accomplish it by."

What you have done (in the amount of time it takes to write up a shopping list) is more than what 95 percent of your competition will ever do in their entire lives, but it's not enough. Having a destination is useless unless you also have a road map. It's the same with a goal. You need a plan that states, "These are the specific steps I will take to reach my destination within the designated time frame." Without the plan you are directionless.

In the book *Alice's Adventures in Wonderland*, by Lewis Carroll, Alice comes to a fork in the road. Having no idea which fork to take, she encounters the Cheshire Cat, who asks Alice where she wants to end up. Alice answers that she has no idea where she's going, to which the Cheshire Cat replies, "In that case, either fork will do."

Everyone who has ever been successful has had a plan, whether it be a general sending troops into battle with a battle plan (do you really think a general would address his troops and say, "They're over that hill somewhere, just go get 'em"?) or a football coach preparing his team by formulating a game plan (no, coaches don't just gather their players together and say, "Hell, we're better than them, just go out and kick some butt").

The U.S. Small Business Administration will tell you the single biggest reason small businesses fail is they did not have a written business plan.

What's amazing is how many salespeople will agree about the importance of a plan and yet never bother to have one, whether it is for their life, career, or business. They'll tell you they're experienced enough to know what to do without having to bother writing one up.

But let me ask you this: Have ever had a house custom built? If you did, I'll bet you hired an architect and had him draw up a set of plans. But why? Didn't you have an experienced builder? Couldn't an experienced builder say to you, "Listen, I just figured out a great way to save you money. Let's dump the architect, you don't need one. I'm an experienced builder. I've been building houses for twenty years. See all those houses over there? I built all of them. I could build your house from memory. So just tell me what you want and I'll do it for you."

Would you do it? Sure, only if you were an idiot. You know what, I'll bet there's a chance that builder *could* build a house from memory, but would you want to take that chance?

The plan is the indispensable piece of the puzzle, because the plan is the magic formula that far too many people are looking for. The plan answers the age-old question that so many people have when it comes to goal setting: "How do I keep the motivation going?"

I often have people tell me, "When I first set a goal, I'm real excited by it. I immediately start working toward it. But then, maybe a few weeks or a few months into it, I start to lose the excitement. How do I keep the motivation going?" The answer is the plan.

When you have a goal and no plan here is what happens.

Point A ————————————————————→ Point B

You're starting at point A and looking to end up at point B. Without a plan, with no road map to get you from point A to point B, every day when you get up the only thing you are giving yourself to focus on is the end result. It doesn't matter whether that end result is 1, 2, 3, 5 or *ten years* down the road; it is the only thing you have to focus on.

You start out very motivated and working toward it, but sooner or later you're going to say, "It seems like I've been working toward this for a very long time and it doesn't look like I'm getting any closer." Can you hear the frustration in that comment? Once frustration starts to set in, what do you think will eventually happen? That's right, you'll give up. And the only time you ever fail is when you give up.

What the plan does is take the big goal and break it up into smaller, easier to accomplish goals, or steps. Once you have done that, once you've created that road map, look what happens. (Think of the stars as the steps of the plan—or your potential stopping-off points.)

Point A   *   *   *   *   *   *   *   *   Point B

Now every morning when you wake, you no longer have to focus on an end result that could be years down the road; you only have to focus on the next step. Since that next step is so much easier to accomplish and can be accomplished so much quicker than the end result, what will happen is you'll work toward it, accomplish it, and how do you think you'll feel when you do? That's right, you'll feel *great*! And if you feel great about what you've just accomplished, what do you think you'll do? Right again, you'll keep going!

You see, as long as you keep going, there's no way you can fail, because you'll eventually get there. Now, once you've accomplished that first step, you only have to focus on the next step. The only time you ever have to focus on the end result is when that becomes the next step and, at that point, it's so much easier to accomplish.

As you can see, by giving you the chance to accomplish small goals on a regular basis, the plan helps you create the "habit of accomplishment," thereby helping build a tremendous amount of confidence.

✍️ SALES TIP

Far too many salespeople fail because they claim they lack confidence. However, confidence only comes from doing. How can you be confident in your ability to do anything if you've never done it? Confidence is strictly a by-product of action.

There is a basic progression to achieving confidence. It is "commitment, courage, confidence." In other words, my *commitment* to the fact that this is what I want and need to do gives me the *courage* to act. Once I've acted, I've begun to develop *confidence*.

Do you remember your first cold call? Were you nervous, were you scared and just a bit (if not a lot) apprehensive? But you went ahead and did it. Why? Because the commitment to the job gave you the courage to act, and once it was done you probably said, "Hey, that wasn't so bad, now I know I can do it again."

In Chapter 3 I wrote that successful salespeople have written goals and strategic plans for their lives, careers, and businesses. When it comes right down to it, successful salespeople plan everything. The reason the top 10 percent outsell the middle 80 percent is they leave nothing to chance. They don't just have a sales plan, they have an activity plan. They plan their sales calls; they plan their prospecting calls; they even plan what they're going to say and what the prospect or client is going to say or might object to. The professional salesperson even plans out what he will say to turn around a prospect or client's objection.

Let's look at some of these plans and why they're so effective.

The Sales Plan

Most salespeople have a sales plan. The successful ones create their own. The rest get theirs from management. When successful salespeople create their own sales plan it's based on what they want to accomplish and the lifestyle they want for their families and themselves. The salesperson who receives a sales plan from management gets one that's based on what someone else wants. What if you get a sales plan from management and you achieve those goals, but it doesn't yield you the results or income *you* really wanted? When salespeople are allowed to set their own goals, they usually set higher goals than what management would have.

The Activity Plan

I believe this is far more important than the sales plan and yet it's one that hardly any salespeople bother to formulate—except, of course, the successful ones. There are three reasons why an activity plan is critical.

1. If you ask any sales executive in the world to name the biggest problem they have with their sales force, the vast majority will say, "They don't see enough people." They're not prospecting enough.

2. It's the only way to handle rejection. The biggest reason salespeople don't see or talk to enough people is simple: fear of rejection. They're afraid someone is going to say no. You know what? They're right, someone is going to say no. You know what else? Who the hell cares? Someone has to say no. I'll guarantee, if you have never heard the word "no" in your sales career, then you have definitely never heard the word, "yes."

3. If you generate activity on a consistent, everyday basis, guess what you'll end up with? As my 14-year-old daughter would say, "Duh," you'll end up with *sales*.

✍ SALES TIP

Let's get this out of the way right up front: Rejection stinks. Any sales trainer who tells you "Don't take it personally, just let it roll off your back," is two things: (1) an idiot, and (2) someone who has never been in the trenches. Until you've driven two hours to an appointment only to have some jerk not show up, or gotten the runaround from one of those "I've gotta think about it" prospects, don't even begin to teach how to handle rejection.

I've been in sales for over 30 years and I still slam down the phone and say, "You dirty _____!" You know why? Because I care! Rejection *is* personal. Everything in life is personal. If I said to you, "Don't take this personally, but. . . . ," no matter what I say next, you're going to take it personally.

There is only one way to handle rejection: You have to know how much rejection you need. If you know how many no's it takes to get to a yes, it will be that much easier to deal with the rejection, and make it a lot less scary. That is why you need an activity plan.

An activity plan will allow you to track your activity in the following six categories.

1. How many times have I dialed the phone?
2. How many decisions makers have I spoken to?
3. How many appointments did I set?
4. How many face to face presentations did I make?
5. How many sales did I close?
6. How much money did I make from each sale?

If you keep track of information like this on a daily basis, total it on a weekly basis, and add up your total numbers every quarter, you'll start to see averages appear. Every salesperson has an average (or their "a lot"):

- The average number of dials it takes to reach a decision maker.

- The average number of conversations with decision makers to land an appointment.

- The percentage of appointments that get cancelled.

- The ratio of closings to appointments.

- The average amount of dollars earned per sale.

I realize that not all salespeople use the phone to set appointments. Some cold-canvass and knock on doors. Just substitute "knocks" for "dials." Some sell right over the phone; in that case, leave out the "appointments" part of your tracking.

In addition, there are many salespeople who do not sell on commission. If that describes you, instead of tracking the amount of money that goes into your pocket as a result of each sale, track the total dollar amount of each sale, so you know how much money you're bringing in to the company—per sale and in total volume.

But however you do it, an activity plan is crucial because what the numbers eventually tell you is how much activity you have to generate every single day in order to earn the amount of money you need to earn.

If you knew what all your ratios were in the six categories just listed, that would break down right to how many times you physically needed to dial the phone each day. In other words, in every category you could figure out how many "no's" you would need to get a "yes." With that information, don't you think it would be that much easier to handle the rejection? I guarantee you'll still hate it, but at least you won't be as afraid of it. And it's the fear of rejection that stops most salespeople, just as fear of failure is the world's biggest obstacle to success.

A Calling Plan

This is also known as a script. I know what you're thinking: "This guy must be nuts. I'm a professional. I'm not about to use a script. Anytime I've ever listened to a salesperson using a script, it sounded so phony. It sounded canned, like they were reading from it. When I'm on the phone with a prospect or in front of someone, I want it to sound like me and fit my personality. I can't do that with a script."

Okay, that's almost a valid complaint, but let me ask you one question. Have you ever been to a Broadway show or any other form of live theatre? Do you think they used a script? I'm sure they did. But did it sound like a script? Did it sound phony or canned, like they were reading from it? By the way, if it did, you got ripped off.) But I'll bet it didn't, and do you know why?

Because they practiced, they rehearsed, hour upon hour, every single day! Because they are professionals—just like you're supposed to be.

Professionals practice. Professional athletes, musicians, actresses, and actors practice every day.

The top surgeons and doctors constantly read journals to keep up with the latest advances in their field. How would you like to be lying on the operating table and overhear the surgeon say, "Whoa, look at this, never saw this before. Oh well, let's just wing it."

The top accountants stay abreast of all the latest tax laws so they can constantly advise their clients.

THE SEVENTH ROCK-SOLID RULE FOR ACHIEVING SALES SUCCESS

Successful salespeople practice and prepare. They practice their presentations and prepare for every appointment.

If you were in attendance on the first day of rehearsal for any Broadway show it would sound horrible because they'd be reading through the script. Only after weeks or months of daily rehearsals does it cease to sound like a script. Plus, since they now know it so well, the actors and actresses can tailor that script to their personalities. How can you tailor your script or sales presentation to your personality if you've never practiced it?

Most salespeople never practice. They believe if they wing it, they're being more spontaneous. All they're being is unprepared. One of my favorite lines I hear from salespeople when I ask them to practice is, "I practice, every time I'm on the phone or in front of a prospect or client; I'm working on getting better."

Okay, let's try this on for size. You and your spouse decide to go to New York City on vacation. The first thing you want to do is go to a real Broadway show, because you've never been to one. You purchase great seats to one of the best shows on Broadway and spend over $100 per ticket.

The night of the show the two of you go out for a nice dinner, then on to the theater. You sit down in your $100-plus seats and all of a sudden the actors and actresses come out on stage to make this announcement: "Folks, we're sorry to say we just got handed this script today so we haven't had a chance to rehearse. But don't worry, we're professionals; we've been doing this for years, so we're just going to wing it. Enjoy the show."

What would you do? I don't know about you, but I'd be banging on that box office door looking to get my money back.

The funny thing is, salespeople say pretty much the same thing in every phone conversation with a prospect, and many of the same things in their presentations. Yet every time they do it they have to think about what they're going to say next because they have never written it down and never planned it out.

When you plan out exactly what you're going to say, and practice it before you meet prospects, you don't have to think about what you're going to say next while you're speaking. This allows you to do something very important: *listen!*

Planning your presentations ahead of time also allows you to plan ahead for any objections you might hear. Amazingly enough, salespeople hear the same objections all the time (too expensive; send me information; I've got to think about it; we already use someone else; the last salesperson didn't service us properly), yet, with the exception of the 10 percent at the top, they never seem to be ready to turn them around.

Follow this logic: What if you were to list the five most common objections you hear, along with turnarounds you would use to counter them, and then practice them religiously? Do you think it would help? Do you think you would be more spontaneous and not have to think about what you wanted to say? Better yet, do you think it would improve your sales effort?

There are not many things more important to your sales success than having a plan. It helps you to constantly outprepare your competition, which gives you an excellent chance of winning.

Jascha Heifetz was considered by many to be the greatest violinist of all time. Even more amazing, he held that top spot for more than 50 years. He died in December 1987 at the age of 86. His obituary appeared on the front page of the *New York Times*. I remember that as I read it, one paragraph just jumped out at me:

It amused him that people expressed surprise that he still needed to practice after fifty years of work. He said, "If I don't practice for one day, I know it; two days, the critics know it; three days, the public knows it."

Guess what? Your public, your clients and prospects, know it too. They know when you don't feel like being there. They know when you're not prepared and haven't done your homework. Successful professional salespeople practice and prepare.

7

The Three Components of an Effective Written Plan

A plan is a list of actions arranged in whatever sequence is thought likely to achieve an objective.

—John Argenti, author, founder of
the Strategic Planning Society

Before we get into the components of an effective plan and get down to actually formulating your action plans, I want you to go back to the list of goals you set at the end of Chapter 4 and designate three goals you would like to start working on today. Do it by numbering them 1, 2, and 3.

Rather than have you form action plans for all the goals you set, let's just work on three. My reasons for this are simple:

- Change is scary and most people resist. Most people do the same thing every day whether it works or not, because it's comfortable. Therefore, to ask you to break out of your comfort zone and do something you might not be used to doing (setting goals and creating action plans) is stupid on my part and a waste of everyone's time. I don't care how much you do, I just care that you do something. Because I know if I can just expand your comfort zone by getting you to work on three goals, you might see it's not as hard as you thought, and it also might work. This will give you the incentive to eventually work on all the goals you wrote down.

- Small changes, implemented on an everyday basis, will always yield great results. Working on three goals is a small change for you. In today's world, if you ask a person to do something that is the least bit difficult, instead of trying to work through it, they just won't do it. What I'm asking you to do is so easy, you have no excuse not to do it.

By the way, if you already write down goals and develop action plans on a regular basis, don't stop at three goals. If you have more than that, do them all.

Now that you've designated the three goals you want to work on, let's look at the three key components of an effective action plan.

An Effective Plan Is Expressed in Continuous Action

This means that you take your goal and break it down into as frequent an action as possible. You want to be able to take a one-year goal, for example, and break it down into monthly, weekly, or preferably daily actions.

The system you want to use is something I call "a little bit a lot, not a lot a little bit." By breaking your goal down into the most frequent tasks possible, once again, you're giving yourself the opportunity to create a good habit and not forcing yourself to do more than you would want to do at any one time.

Let's say your goal was to lose 30 pounds in a year and get in shape. First of all, you would adjust your plan so that all you had to do was lose 2.5 pounds a month, which for some reason seems easier than losing 30 pounds in a year.

Next, would you start exercising three to four times a week for 30 minutes each time or would you exercise once a week for two hours? Obviously, you would choose the former, but that's not what most people do.

Most people, even though they haven't exercised in years, would first go out and spend hundreds of dollars on exercise wear (when it cost $29.95 it was called "sweats"). Then they drop another $150 on athletic footwear (when that was $29.95 it was called "sneakers"). They then go to a health club where they sign a contract for $17 a month for the next 325 months, because they are convinced that after not having exercised for years they will now go religiously.

Why do you think most health clubs oversell their memberships? Because they know most people won't show up. They also charge a low monthly fee spread out over years, because they know if you saw what it cost up front, you would be a lot more hesitant to sign up. Have you ever noticed when health clubs are busiest? Sure, January, because everyone is gung ho about their New Year's resolutions. Believe me, by March you'll be working out in private, except for maybe May or June, when some people come back briefly for swimsuit season.

But these people are convinced they're going to go all the time. So next, they sign up with a private trainer named Hans (whose mentor was probably Attila the Hun). They go the first time and work out on the torture machines for two hours. The next morning they wake in pain, walking like Quasimodo (the hunchback of Notre Dame, in case you don't recognize the name). What do you think their attitude is toward exercise now? Right, horrible; they hate it and dread it. Do you think their attitude might have been different if they had done 20 or 30 minutes of light exercise three or four times a week in the first few weeks? No doubt they would have seen results, and they probably would have looked forward to exercising a heck of a lot more.

It's the same thing with sales. Far too many salespeople start the year on the wrong side of the equation. They say, "This year if I make a lot of calls, I'll make a lot of sales." They come to work on January 2 to start the year, and the first three people they call say, "Drop dead!" Guess what—their year is over.

The successful salesperson starts from the correct side of the equation. She might say to herself, "How much money do I need to earn this year to support the lifestyle my family and I choose to live?" (I mean everything, including the amount of money you need to sock away for the future). Once she has that amount sorted out, it's easy to devise a plan expressed in continuous action that will help her achieve the goal.

Let's say, for argument's sake, she decides she needs to earn $100,000 this year to support her and her family's lifestyle. She thinks to herself, "That's a lot of money. I've never earned that much before." But, because she is a professional, she has kept good records and has tracked her activity. She figured out that, on the average (and every salesperson has an average), she earns $1,000 commission for every sale. Now she thinks to herself, "I don't have to earn $100,000; I just have to close 100 sales, or, better yet, 2 sales a week."

But, "Hold it a second," she says, "it's not always within my power to close a sale." Sometimes the prospect says no. Sometimes they say something even worse: "I have to think about it." But not always; sometimes they do buy and since she's a professional who keeps records, she knows that she closes on one of every three face-to-face presentations.

Time out for a sales rant.

I hate "I've got to think about it." It usually means they're too weeny to say no, or too scared to say yes. I like to tell prospects, "No is the second-best thing you can tell me, because at least if you say no, I know enough to move on."

Actually, "I've got to think about it" means you once again have to go over everything you told them that they've already agreed to, to find out where the fear lies. If you leave and have to follow up on an "I've gotta think about it," rest assured they're not going to think about it, and even if they do, they're not going to remember much of what you told them.

Now let's look: She doesn't have to earn any money; she doesn't even have to close any sales. All she has to do is make six face-to-face presentations a week. Hey, this job is starting to get a lot easier.

But wait, it's not always within the salesperson's power to make sure the prospect or client shows. Some of them don't show; some of them cancel. But not all of them. And because this young lady is a true pro and has kept great records, she knows that she holds on to 75 percent of her appointments.

So hold it—she doesn't have to make any money; she doesn't have to sell anything; hell, she doesn't even have to see these people.

All she would need to do is set up eight appointments a week. Those eight appointments would yield six face-to-face presentations, leading to two sales at $1,000 commission each, or $2,000 a week. and $100,000 for the year.

✍ SALES TIP

Ever wonder why you get so many appointment cancellations? I wondered, too, for a long time, until one day I was working with a young salesperson who was having that exact problem. He was getting an inordinate number of appointments cancelled. I finally had him account for every minute of his day and then it hit me: He was calling to confirm.

Before you start thinking to yourself, "This guy is definitely a few cards short of a full deck," let me explain.

When you call to confirm an appointment, you probably say, "Ms. Worthington (don't you get sick of people always using Smith and Jones?), I just wanted to make sure we're still on for today." Do you know what you have you just told Ms. Worthington by asking that question? You've told her it's okay to cancel. You might as well have just said, "Ms. Worthington, I just want to let you know that this is your last shot. If you didn't know before that it was okay to cancel, I'm telling you now and if you want, you're off the hook."

When you say, "Just want to make sure we're on for today," does the person on the other end ever say, "I'm glad you called"? I'll bet at that moment, *you're* not too glad you called. Don't confirm, *just go!*

The only way I'll ever tell you to confirm is if you can open your appointment calendar and show me that you just can't fit anyone else in. Other than that, just go! The vast majority of salespeople don't have nearly enough appointments.

I know, you're saying to yourself, "But what if I drive over there and they don't show up?" Great! You can now use one of the greatest motivators in the area of sales: guilt! Leave a note stating, "I was here for our appointment. Hope nothing bad happened to you or your family and that everything is okay." Guaranteed you'll get another appointment, and your odds of closing just got a hell of a lot better.

So the young lady who wants to earn the $100,000 now realizes that all she has to do is set up eight appointments a week. But again, getting a decision maker to agree to see you is not 100 percent within a salesperson's control. Some people will say no, some will stall you, some might even hang up on you—but not all of them. Since our salesperson in this scenario is a true professional and, I repeat, she keeps great records, she knows that one of every five decision makers she speaks to gives her an appointment.

Now let me get this straight. Don't have to make any money; don't have to sell anything; don't have to see anyone; don't even have set up any appointments. I just have to speak to 40 decision makers a week.

But, you know, not everyone gets on the phone. Sometimes I end up speaking with a secretary or other gatekeepers. Sometimes I get voice mail. (By the way, I like voice mail. You can leave exactly the kind of message you want, without someone misinterpreting it. Also, to answer a question I get often, yes, I do leave messages, and you know why? Because I guarantee if you don't, no one will ever call you back.) Sometimes if I call someone at a home office I might even end up speaking to a nine-year-old kid.

But we know that doesn't always happen. In fact, our $100,000 salesperson has figured out from her records that one out of every three times she physically dials the phone she gets to a decision maker.

So now hold on a second: Don't have to make any money; don't have to sell anything; don't have to see anyone or set up appointments; hell, I don't even have to talk to these people. All I have to do is dial the phone 120 times a week or 24 times a day, because if I do that:

- I'll speak to 8 decision makers a day or 40 a week.
- I'll set up eight appointments a week and actually hold six of them.
- Those six face-to-face presentations will yield me two sales (on average) and put $2,000 a week in my pocket.
- That translates to $100,000 a year.

Now how motivated do you think that young lady is to make the calls? You're right: She's a lunatic, because she knows that every day she comes to work and gets to 24 calls she's getting that much closer to what she wants. That's continuous action.

✐ SALES TIP

As you can see from the scenario described in this section, the generation of activity is the only part of the sales process that is 100 percent within the salesperson's control. Every other part of the process—getting to speak to the decision maker, setting up an appointment, holding on to it, closing the sales—you need someone else to agree with you. The generation of activity is all up to you.

The only reason a salesperson would not be generating the proper amount of activity is if she's just being lazy.

An Effective Plan Is Broken Down into Accomplishable Steps

When formulating your action plans, be sure to make the first few steps of the plan so easy to accomplish that you have no excuse not to do it. Why would you want to make it tough on yourself?

Let's go back to Motivation 101. What do they always say? "The toughest step of any journey is . . ." Right, the first step. Well, if the first step is so hard to take, why do so many people insist on making it the hardest to accomplish? Why not make it the easiest to accomplish?

After all, the whole idea of the first few steps is not to accomplish the whole goal, but just to get you rolling. If you make them easy to accomplish, you'll be more willing to take them, you'll be racking up accomplishments left and right, and you'll start saying, "Hey this isn't so tough, I'm going to keep going." Remember, you only fail if you give up, so the key is to ask yourself, "What can I do for myself that's going to make it easy for me to keep going? Because I know as long as I keep going, I'll eventually get to where I want to be."

Remember, you're just trying to expand your comfort zone gradually, not bust out of it. What you're trying to figure out is, "How much can I do every day without really hating it, getting sick of it, or wanting to avoid doing it?" But in order to do this, you first have to figure out where you are right now.

Let's take the example of our $100,000 salesperson. She found out that she needed to make 24 calls a day, every day, or 120 a week, to reach her goal. But what happens if, currently, she's only generating 20 prospecting calls a week, or just 4 a day? Do you really think she's going to go from 20 calls a week to 120 a week overnight? It's possible, but I'd hate to see the effect it would have on her.

Going from 20 calls a week to 120 the next week means she would be making 100 more calls a week than she was used to making. It would also mean she'd be dealing with around 98 more rejections a week than she was used to.

What do you think her reaction would be? Well, assuming she didn't end up going into a catatonic state and being dragged out of there feet first, my guess would be she would dread prospecting.

Time out for another rant.

One of my pet peeves with sales managers is phone-a-thons. That's the practice where they get their sales force together and say, "From now on, every Tuesday you're all going to get on the phone and make one hundred calls. But after we're done I'm going to treat everyone to pizza." Whoopee—kill me now.

What do you think is going on in the minds of these salespeople every Monday night? They're either coming down with hives from the stress of thinking about Tuesday, or they just dread it. Why not just have them make 20 calls a day every day, which is much easier to deal with, or, better yet, follow the suggestion I'm about to give for our $100,000 salesperson.

Instead of her going from 4 calls a day to 20 calls a day immediately, do you think she could make 5 calls a day, comfortably? I'll bet she could. Once you find what your level is and how much activity you generate every day, just increase by one and do that amount every day for a month.

After a month, increase by one more call per day and do that every day for a month. Now while it might not seem like much, going from four calls a day to five would increase her daily activity by 25 percent, which could also increase her sales by 25 percent. After a month, when she goes from five calls a day to six, she's increased her activity by another 20 percent. She will eventually reach 20 calls a day and she'll do it at her pace, while developing the habit of daily activity.

As I wrote in Chapter 6, most sales executives agree that the single biggest problem they have with their salespeople is they don't talk to and see enough prospects. Because of their ability to break down their plans into continuous action and accomplishable steps, successful salespeople give us the next rule.

THE EIGHTH ROCK-SOLID RULE FOR ACHIEVING SALES SUCCESS
Successful salespeople see and talk to more people than anyone else and get more people to say no to them.

Many years ago I was keynoting the annual sales meeting for a large light bulb manufacturer. The night before my speech I attended their annual awards dinner. If you've ever attended one, you know they're pretty much like Little League banquets: Everyone gets a trophy.

The most interesting part of this dinner was the award for the Salesperson of the Year. Incredibly, it went to a rookie—someone in his first year in sales.

Now I'm watching this young guy walk up to the stage, and I must admit he looked like a bit of a dope. He also looked like he got dressed in the dark. When the president of the company handed him the award he asked him to say a few words and tell us all the secret of his success.

The young man looked at him and said, "I don't know, my manager told me not to come back every day until I saw 30 people and that's what I did." The president of the company, not seeming to believe him, said again, "Come on, don't be shy, tell us your secret." Again the young man said, "I don't know, my manager told me not to come back every day until I saw 30 people and that's what I did."

Amazingly enough, this young man was so dumb and so naive, he didn't know he wasn't supposed to see anyone. The coffee-cup brigade and the 10-year veterans who are really one-year veterans multiplied by 10 hadn't gotten to him yet. I'm only sorry I didn't follow up a year later to see what happened.

**An Effective Plan Gives You the Ability to
Measure Your Progress Every Step of the Way**

There's a real good reason why your plan needs to enable you to measure progress every step of the way: so that you know you've made some.

Do you really believe that you can actually see, touch, or feel the little bits of progress you'll make along the way, unless you could quantify it on paper? Let me show you what I mean.

Let's say you've set a goal that you expect to achieve in five years, or 60 months, but you've given yourself no ability to measure your progress. You're real gung ho at the beginning and work toward this goal every day.

Assume that after three months you're 5 percent closer to your goal, and three months into a 60 month goal 5 percent progress is right on target. However, if you have no ability to measure progress, would you really know you were 5 percent closer to your goal? I doubt it. How could you possibly know? Five percent is not a big change. In fact, what would you probably be saying to yourself at this point? Most likely, "I've been working toward this goal for three months and I don't feel as though I'm making any progress. I feel like I'm still on square one."

Sounds like someone's getting frustrated, and the next step after frustration is giving up, which, as we now know, is the only time you fail. I wonder how many times you've given up on something because you didn't give yourself the opportunity to see the progress you were making and you just assumed you hadn't made any.

For a great example of the ability to measure your progress, let's look at my two favorite salespeople, salesperson A and salesperson B. We can see from the accompanying chart that they both have the same goal for the year: Close 144 sales. Salesperson B is one of those 10-year veterans who has one year of experience multiplied by 10, plus he's a member in good standing of the coffee cup brigade. He has decided he doesn't need a plan. He states, "Don't worry about me. I've been around ten years. Just tell me what to do and I'll do it."

Salesperson A, on the other hand, isn't quite as confident. She says, "One hundred and forty-four sales? I've never done that before. I better put together a plan." So she does and, after analyzing it, figures out that she really doesn't have to close 144 sales. She just needs to close 12 sales a month.

Goal for the Year: 144 Sales Each

	Salesperson A	Salesperson B
December	12	
November	12	
October	12	
September	12	
August	12	
July	12	
June	12	
May	12	
April	12	
March	12	
February	12	
January	12	

Well January comes and goes, and guess what? Salesperson A has closed 12 sales. What do you think she's saying to herself? "I did it. I reached my goal. I'm right on target." What's her next goal? That's right: 12.

Now let's see what happened to salesperson B. By the end of January he, too, has closed 12 sales. What do you think he's saying to himself at that point? You got it: "Oh my god, 132 to go!"

Somewhere around April, salesperson B will be telling anyone who'll listen, "I don't think this goal is very realistic." Salesperson B is also one of those people who doesn't understand that in order to be in control of your destiny, you first have to *take* control of your destiny. However, without a plan, salesperson B has no chance.

You see, salesperson B is one of those people who tell me what a great fourth-quarter salesperson they are. As soon as I hear that, I know I'm speaking to someone who sleepwalked through the first three quarters. What really gets me is when a manager says, "We're a great December office." I know from experience that means that all the turkeys in that office don't wake up until Thanksgiving to realize they're 70 percent behind quota.

Salesperson B is now in a position where one bad day in December can equal one bad year. What should happen if there's a freak snowstorm in December and he can't get out? One bad day equals one bad year. What if his car breaks down one day in December and he isn't able to see clients? Again, one bad day equals one bad year. Or maybe he comes down with the flu in December and is laid up for a couple of days. Once again, one bad day equals one bad year.

Then in January, salesperson B becomes one of those people who could have bought a building 30 years ago for $9.00. He'll say, "I could have made quota, but how was I supposed to know it was going to snow? (This clown probably lives in Chicago!) I'm supposed to know my car is going to break down? I'm supposed to know I'm going to get the flu?"

You know, he's right—he's not supposed to know that was going to happen. But he is supposed to know that *something's* going to happen, and you why? Because it always does.

If salesperson A experiences a freak snowstorm, comes down with the flu, or has her car break down, her year is not ruined, because for her one bad day only equals one bad day. You see, salesperson A realized that the time to start worrying about December was not on Thanksgiving day, but way back in the first quarter when she could still do something about it.

I think the story that best depicts the importance of continuous-action, accomplishable steps, and the ability to measure progress took place in North Africa in 1943 during World War II.

At that time, Field Marshall Rommel, the German tank commander, had just finished blitzing his way across North Africa. He left in his wake two badly beaten and demoralized armies, American and British. These soldiers were so beaten they no longer had any sense of self-worth or self-esteem. Their uniforms were filthy and, in turn, their camps were filthy.

Into this mess stepped two great leaders. General Patton took command of the American troops in North Africa and Field Marshall Montgomery assumed command of the British troops.

I don't know if you know anything about Patton and Montgomery, but I can tell you they were as different as night and day. On top of that, they didn't particularly like each other. Montgomery thought Patton was an out-of-control American cowboy and Patton thought Montgomery was a wuss.

However, as different as they were, they both faced the same problem. What was the long-term, ultimate goal? Win the war, of course. But do you really think you could take troops in this condition and win a war? Patton and Montgomery knew they first needed some short-term goals.

One was to get the troops to believe they could win the war. Another, even shorter-term goal was to get them to believe they could do anything. Amazingly, they both collaborated on the same solution.

All they asked was that each soldier do three things every day:

1. Wear a clean uniform.
2. Do 20 push-ups.
3. Run one mile.

Now I know that doesn't seem like much, but what did these two great leaders know? They knew they first had to build the confidence of the men, and when you are achieving your goals on a continuous, daily basis, your confidence starts to sky rocket. That's what happened.

As the troops became more and more confident, Patton and Montgomery gradually increased the difficulty of the tasks. Eventually, they built a lean, mean fighting machine. And if you don't know how it ended, we won.

Continuous action, accomplishable steps, and the ability to measure our progress every step of the way—that's what makes up an effective action plan.

Now you're ready to formulate your plan, and this is what I want you to do. On the accompanying forms, take the three goals you chose to work on and write them out, in full, one per form. Also, notice the place for you to plug in the year you intend to achieve this goal. This is critical since, as stated before, a goal is a dream with a deadline.

Once you've done that, go to it. List the steps you will take to achieve each one of your three goals. Take some time and do it now. One piece of advice: As you're doing this, try to visualize yourself working toward that goal. If you can see yourself doing it, it will be easier to come up with the steps you need to take. This is it—this is your plan. I told you I'd get you here, and I did. The rest is up to you.

Goal 1

Year of completion: _____

Steps:

1.

2.

3.

4.

5.

6.

7.

8.

9.

10.

Goal 2

Year of completion: _____

Steps:

  1.

  2.

  3.

  4.

  5.

  6.

  7.

  8.

  9.

10.

Goal 3

Year of completion: _____

Steps:

1.

2.

3.

4.

5.

6.

7.

8.

9.

10.

8 | Acting on Your Plan: You Have Twenty-Four Hours to Act on a Good Idea

Never mistake motion for action.
—Ernest Hemingway

Everybody has good ideas. The world is filled with people who can come up with new and better ways to do things. However, the difference between a good idea and a successful idea is *action*.

I wonder how many times you've come up with a great idea, did nothing about it, and then a year or two later saw it somewhere else? When you saw it what did you say? "Hey, that was my idea!" Yeah, so what? Everyone has good ideas, but only the successful people act on them.

If you want to better understand the power of action, read *They Made America*, Harold Evans' book on innovation. He shows how practical innovation more than anything else is the reason the United States achieved preeminence while other well-endowed landmasses lagged or failed.

Mr. Evans writes that innovation is not simply invention; it is inventiveness put to use (or, in other words, acted upon). Originality is not the prime factor; effectiveness is. Some examples from the book:

- Bill Gates has never invented any important, original software. The BASIC programming language Gates and Paul Allen first adopted for the personal computer in 1974 was invented 10 years earlier by two Dartmouth professors. DOS was based on Tim Paterson's QDOS.

- The radar system, penicillin, the first commercial application of the computer, and the jet engine—all these British inventions were superseded by the innovative energies of Americans and transformed into major American-driven industries.

- Cyrus McCormick was not the only farmer to invent a reaper, but he was the one who initiated the financing mechanisms that made it possible for hundreds of thousands of farmers to afford the invention.

THE NINTH ROCK-SOLID RULE FOR ACHIEVING SALES SUCCESS

Successful salespeople take action. They don't wait for someone else to do it for them.

As the title of this chapter states, you have 24 hours to act on a good idea. If you do nothing about a good idea within 24 hours, rest assured, it's dead.

Now, I'm not saying you have to do *everything* about a good idea within 24 hours, but you have to take at least one action step, if for nothing else than to keep the excitement going.

You know as well as I do that we're most excited about our good ideas when we first get them. The longer we wait to do something about an idea, the less excited we get. In fact, we probably spend more time talking ourselves out of it or letting other people tell us why it's a lousy idea.

Right now you have in your possession a very valuable and powerful weapon: your action plan. However, it will only work if you make it work by acting on it. Let me tell you seven things you can do to make this plan work.

1. First, make a copy of the page where you wrote down all your goals and make a copy of the three forms where you created action plans for your three most important goals.

2. Take these pages and post them someplace where you can see them every day. If you don't want anyone else to see them, a good place is the inside of your closet door at home. I assume you open your closet door every day, unless you just toss your clothes on the floor. Posting them up where

you can see them every day keeps the goals fresh in your mind and makes them dominant in your thoughts. Napoleon Hill, author of *Think and Grow Rich*, stated, "We are what we think about all day long," and "We move toward our most dominant thoughts."

3. I believe in posting goals up where anyone can see them because "you never know." In fact, if you want to get to your goals even faster, tell everyone you know, even people who you would never expect to be able to help you, because you never know, help can come from some of the most unexpected places.

In my early days as a speaker, one of my goals was to produce a good promotional videotape that would help me market my services as a speaker. My one problem was that it was going to cost me thousands of dollars that I didn't have. So I just started telling everyone I knew about my goal. One of the people I told was my best friend, Alan. Why, I had no idea, since, at the time, Alan worked as the director of one of the largest, if not *the* largest, mental hospitals in the United States. It must have just come up in passing. Alan, to my shock, said, "Why didn't you come to me right away? I have a complete video production facility on the grounds of the hospital. Come to the hospital, we'll put together an audience (of staff, not patients), you do a speech for us for free, we'll shoot the video for you, and you can have the master." I got myself a free promotional video, all because I told everyone I knew about my goal—and you never know.

4. Once you have your plan posted up, it's important to review it on a regular basis. I suggest you review your plan every quarter, if for no other reason than to make sure the goals you set for yourself are still important to you. Let's face it, people change and priorities change. What's important to

you today might not be important a year from now. If that should happen, what do you do about the goal? Change it, of course, or get rid of it. Remember, this plan is yours; it can change. It was written in pen or pencil on a sheet of paper. It wasn't carved into a block of stone with a chisel. It can change.

5. What do you do if you get to reach your deadline and you haven't yet achieved the goal? Kill yourself, of course! No, of course not—just move back the deadline! Remember, it's *yours*! It can change. Believe me, the goal-setting police are not going to bash in your door, grab you by the neck, and say, "Okay pal, you're coming with us." That's not going to happen. I'm amazed at people who say ridiculous things like, "My goal was to lose thirty pounds in a year and I only lost twenty-five. I failed." No! You didn't fail. Just move back the deadline and create a new goal: "I want to lose five pounds in the next three months." The deadline is there to give you a frame of reference and to give you the incentive to get started. It's not there as a punishment, something to flog yourself with should you not achieve your goal in time.

6. What do you do if you happen to achieve all the goals you set for yourself? Stop right there, your life is now over. No! Set some more goals! Create an action plan for each one. Do the same thing to set the new goals that you did to set these. Successful salespeople are always setting and creating new challenges for themselves.

7. Here's a guarantee for you: I guarantee that if you shove this plan into a drawer and never look at it again, it will never work.

Tommy Lasorda, former manager of the Los Angeles Dodgers, used to say there are three kinds of people in the world: Those who make things happen (the top 10 percent), those who watch things happen (middle 80 percent), and those who sit around and say, "What happened?" (the bottom 10 percent).

By the way, the parentheses in that last statement are mine. They point out where the three groups of salespeople fall when it comes to taking action.

Successful salespeople don't wait around for business to fall into their laps. It is not true that if you build a better mousetrap the world will beat a path to your door. You still have to tell the world you exist. Average salespeople assume the clients know they exist.

Here's one for you to roll around in your head: Would you agree there aren't many people in the world who haven't heard of McDonald's or Coca-Cola? If that's the case, then how do you explain the billions of dollars they spend on advertising? Believe me, if Coca-Cola and McDonald's need to tell their customers they're still around, then so do you.

The lack of action on the part of salespeople goes way beyond their lack of prospecting and the fact that they don't have enough appointments. The appalling lack of action shows up in their poor follow-up, which can be the kiss of death for salespeople.

✍ SALES TIP: FOLLOW-UP

This tip could easily qualify as a rant, since salesperson follow-up, or the lack of it, drives me insane. I can't tell you how many salespeople leave huge amounts of business on the table because of their dreadful inability to take action and follow up. Not only don't they get back to you when they say they will, but how many actually stay in touch with their clients after the sale is made? What makes it even worse is that staying in touch with clients and prospects is easier than ever with the invention of e-mail.

Not only does almost every businessperson have an e-mail address, but they're far more likely to read their e-mails and answer them than to answer phone calls or even return your calls. E-mail is one of the greatest nonthreatening ways of staying in touch with clients and prospects.

How hard is it to show up on time? How difficult is it to send a thank you note after a sale or an appointment? Is it really that much of an inconvenience to call someone back when you said you would? Obviously it is, because just by constantly implementing those three action steps, the top 10 percent separate themselves from the 90 percent below them.

When my family and I relocated from New York City to Chapel Hill, my wife and I interviewed salespeople from three different moving companies. Guess which one we hired? The cheapest? No. We gave our business to the one salesperson who showed up on time for our appointment. We figured if they can't even be on time to take our money, what's going to happen once they have our money and our furniture?

One of the salespeople even told us the reason she was late was because she was way too busy with other customers. I asked if that entitled me to a "We're busy" discount, or was I going to pay the same price as the customers she deemed to be more important? And, if so, then why the hell should I care if she's busy?

In 1987 I bought my first life insurance policy. I had delivered a speech to a local agency of a large life insurance company. Let's call them Company A, to protect the stupid. After I was done speaking, a young man approached me and asked if he could speak to me about my life insurance needs. I said, "Fine, give me a call."

He gave me a call and then came over to see my wife and me. He proceeded to sell us a small policy (I had been in business less than a year, so affordability was a problem), then he left—never to be heard from again. I often wonder, why do so many salespeople assume your income or business is never going to go up? Maybe because theirs is not.

A little more than a year later, I was attending a business networking function in Manhattan. A young woman approached me. She was an agent from a different company; let's call them Company B. She asked if she could speak to me about my life insurance needs. I said, "Fine, give me a call."

She gave me a call, came over to see my wife and me, and proceeded to sell me another small policy, though it was bigger than the first one. Afterwards, she left, never to be heard from again.

OKAY, I admit I did stretch the truth about the salesperson from Company A. He did get back to me—more than two and half years after selling me the policy! He phoned me one day and said, "I'd like to speak to you about buying more life insurance." I said, "Too late, I already bought more life insurance." He was mad. He said, "Why didn't you buy it from me? You should have called."

I said, "I should have called you? Hey, listen, pal, if I have to call you and help you sell me life insurance, I want to split the commission." He got mad and hung up. He never wanted to speak to me again—a great sense of loss in my life.

I never again heard from the agent from either Company A or Company B. A year later I found out they both left the insurance industry. They probably thought there was no opportunity to be successful. Of course, you can get that impression if you never follow up with your clients.

By the way, an interesting thing about those two agents leaving the industry: While I had policies on the books with both those companies (I still have the policy from Company A), I've never received a call from an agent with either company. You'd think someone would want to speak to me about buying more insurance.

About two years later, in 1992, I met an agent from another insurance company. Let's call them Company C. He asked if he could speak to me about my life insurance needs and I said, "Fine, give me a call."

In case you're wondering why I always say, "Fine, give me a call," it's because I find it's the easiest way to get rid of mediocre to poor salespeople: Ask them to put forth the slightest effort. I know that most salespeople will never call.

The agent from Company C did call and, over the next two years, through his action, diligence, follow-up, and willingness to fill our needs, sold me five policies totaling $2 million worth of life insurance.

Now here's the best part. My agent from Company C left the insurance industry in 1995. With five policies and $2 million of insurance on the books, I've never received a call from anyone else from Company C.

In 1997, I found a new agent. He's been my agent to this day. I've done more business with him than with any of my other agents. In fact, aside from new policies and other financial products I bought, I also had a couple of term insurance policies with Company C that I cancelled and moved over to my current agent.

Finally, one day a customer service rep from Company C called to inquire why I had cancelled those policies. I told her the new company I was with had far lower premium costs on term insurance, and besides, "I had five policies with your company totaling two million dollars in insurance; my agent left the industry almost three years ago and I've never received a call from anyone in your company."

She replied, "You know, a lot of people are telling us that." At this point, all I could think of were two things:

1. How dumb is she to admit it, and?

2. If you know that, why don't you do something about it?

But of course, that would take action.

Let me tell you one of my philosophies. I honestly, truly believe there is no such thing as a bad idea. I really believe that. To me the only bad ideas are the ones that are not acted upon, or are not acted upon properly. And if you don't believe that there's no such thing as a bad idea, let me give you these four words: *teenage, mutant, ninja, turtles!*

Did you ever hear of a dumber idea than Teenage Mutant Ninja Turtles? That has to be the dumbest idea in the world! For those of you who don't know what they are let me tell you.

They are four little green turtles. Their names are Michelangelo, Leonardo, Raphael, and Donatello. They became mutants from a radioactive canister that fell in the gutter. They live in a sewer; their boss is a rat (the real kind, not your normal, everyday rat of a boss) and they eat nothing but pizza. It is the dumbest idea in the world!

But they started out as a black-and-white comic book in 1984; in 1987 they hit television in an animated cartoon show that lasted for a decade and was then revived in 2003. In 1990 the Turtles starred in a live action movie. Their merchandise sales have included toys, books, games, clothing, underwear, towels, video games, and on and on and on. It became the longest-running fad in American history and they made billions—and it is the *dumbest idea in the world!*

But now let me ask you this. What if someone would have approached you sometime back in the mid to late 1980s and said, "I got the greatest idea in the world! This is so great, you're not gonna believe it. We're gonna make millions! All you gotta do is put in ten thousand dollars and we're rolling. This is so great! Let me tell what it is. Let me tell you what it is!

"Teenage, mutant, ninja turtles! Huh, huh, is that great? I know, I know what you're thinking, but let me tell you what they are. Let me tell you what they are! These are little green turtles that live in a sewer. Their boss is a rat and they eat nothing but pizza. Are you in?!"

What would you have said? Probably "Are you crazy?" You know who else said that? Hasbro—at the time, one of the single largest toy makers in the world. They said, "No one will ever buy little green turtles that live in a sewer." How would you like to be the executive who made that decision?

There is no such thing as a bad idea. But you have to act, you have to take that first step. You have to do something.

9

Persistence: People Don't Fail, They Just Stop Trying

Nothing in the world can take the place of persistence. Talent will not; nothing is more common than unsuccessful men with talent. Genius will not; unrewarded genius is almost a proverb. Education will not; the world is full of educated derelicts. Persistence and determination alone are omnipotent. The slogan "Press on" has solved and always will solve the problems of the human race.

—Calvin Coolidge

Okay, you've seen it. You've seen yourself successful, visualized it, focused, described it, set the goal, and planned it out. You even started, acted, and took that first step. But now we come to the final step of the goal setting process. It is here where the 3 percent who will be great will leave the other 97 percent behind. It is called persistence.

As I've stated throughout this book, people don't fail; they just stop trying. As long as you keep going out there day after day after day, you are constantly giving yourself the opportunity to be successful, to be great, to be the best. The second you stop, you have taken away any opportunity you ever had to be great.

Too many people confuse falling down with failing. When people go ice skating, so many of them judge their proficiency by how many times they fall down. For instance, "How did you do today?" "Great! I only fell once."

Does falling down once really tell us whether a person can skate? How do we know they didn't spend their whole time hanging on to the rail? Or maybe they skate by taking baby steps. Olympic skaters fall; NHL hockey players fall. Why? Because they're not afraid to let go of the proverbial railing. They're more concerned with succeeding than with not falling down.

The point is, in skating as in life, falling down is no measuring stick for either success or failure, mostly because "not falling down" is not the same as success, and "falling down" is not the same as failure.

It is very easy to never fall down: Just don't ever do anything. Never take a risk; never try anything you're not 100 percent certain you'll succeed at, and never go beyond your own self-imposed limitations. Once again, in life and ice skating, fear of falling down (notice I didn't say "fear of failure"—you'll find out why soon) is the biggest obstacle to success.

I said this before and I will say it again: Falling down is not failing. Not getting up is failing. We are so conditioned to equate falling down with failing that many people have become almost nonchalant about it.

For example, many people don't pass the road test when trying for their driver's license. What do they do? They take it again until they pass. Yet even years later when asked how they did on the road test they say, "I failed it the first time." Wrong! You didn't fail it, you just didn't pass it the first time. The proof is that you succeeded in getting a license. The only way you could have failed the road test would be if you didn't take it again after the first try.

This attitude filters right down to our schools. When a child fails to pass a grade, the system claims he failed. However, instead of asking the child to repeat the grade, most school systems will just pass that child on to the next grade, claiming, "We don't feel it's good for the child's self-esteem to leave him back." Right—but it's good for the child's self-esteem to promote him into an even harder grade when he couldn't do the work in the previous grade?

The child will run into the same problems in the next grade and this will just reinforce in the child's mind that he is not capable of doing the work. Eventually this child will get frustrated, not see the point in going on, and drop out. It is then, when that child has stopped trying, that he truly fails.

A child doesn't fail a grade if he doesn't pass the first time but takes it over and succeeds. How can we call that failure? And by getting up after falling down, trying again, and succeeding, isn't that child building real, long-lasting self-esteem?

Of course, you might ask, "How can you expect a child to keep getting up and trying after falling down? How many adults would do that?" To that I can answer, "Only the successful ones."

THE TENTH ROCK SOLID RULE FOR ACHIEVING SALES SUCCESS
Successful salespeople are persistent.

One of the most important things successful salespeople understand is that when a client or prospect says no today, it only means no today. It does not mean no tomorrow, next week, or next month.

What would have happened to Peter Rosengaard (see Chapter 2) if he had stopped after leaving that first message? We know for a fact he never would have closed the $100 million sale and gotten into the *Guinness Book of World Records*.

Just because a prospect isn't interested in seeing you or in hearing about or buying your products or services today, doesn't mean they never will be. There could be numerous reasons why they said no today. Here are just a few examples:

- They could have been having a bad day and would have said no to anything.
- Maybe they haven't set their budgets yet and don't want to see anyone before then.
- They just bought from someone else and you were too late.
- They've been using the same supplier for quite a few years and are very happy with the relationship.

None of these examples stops successful salespeople from ever calling back. In the case of the first one, just call back a few days later. I know what you're thinking, but believe me, they're not going to think you're bugging them. More likely, they won't even remember you called the first time.

With reason number two, just find out when they expect the budgets to be set and call back then. I know that sounds simple, but there are way too many salespeople who think their job ends after the first call.

Reasons three and four are where too many salespeople give up, but if you do, you could be missing out on a great opportunity. First of all, if someone has just bought from your competition or has had a relationship with a competitor for years, that's a good thing—it means they use what you sell and they believe in the value of what you do. They're qualified!

Of course, this doesn't mean that you keep calling every week, but they should be hearing from you at least once a year, because you never know. How do you know they're not going to have a bad experience with the company they just bought from or with the one they've been using for years? Suppliers screw up; hell, everyone screws up.

If you would have called me to sell me life insurance in 1993, I would have told you I had an agent with whom I was very happy. If you recall from Chapter 8, that was the agent from Company C. But if you had continued to follow up with me once a year and called in 1996, right after the agent from Company C had left the industry and I was looking for a new agent, you would have ended up with a lot of business over the next few years.

✍ SALES TIP

Here are a couple of other tips about not giving up:

- Sometimes you just run into people who are a total brick wall. No matter what you do they won't answer your calls, e-mails, or whatever else you use to contact them, and then they finally say to you, "Stop bugging me." I like to use this line I learned many years ago in the garment center: "If you want me to stop bugging you, that's easy—just buy something from me." Don't worry about insulting them. Just remember this: If someone is not going to buy from you for no reason at all, you might as well give them one.

- When someone tells you, "Give me your number and we'll call you when we're ready," use a line we've been using in our office for years. We say, "Don't bother." This immediately puts them into total shock, because they can't believe there's a salesperson in the world who wouldn't want to be called. But you know as well as I do, in most cases, they're never going to call you, so right after you say, "Don't bother," then say, "It's not your responsibility to call me, it's my responsibility to call you." Then set up a time, convenient to all, to follow up, and then do it.

My wife, Linda, takes care of all sales for our speaking business. Over the last 15 years she has compiled a database of companies and people who not only hire professional speakers but whose budget can afford my fee. There are some people she has called for years with no luck, but there are many who, after five years or more of turning us down, hired me to be the keynote speaker at their meeting.

I once heard my friend Bill Brooks, one of America's top sales experts, say, "The key to selling is to be in front of the prospect when he or she is ready to buy. But since we don't necessarily know when that will be, it's a good idea to try to be in front of them as much as possible."

Persistence in sales is very much about follow-up. It's about the ability and willingness to keep your name and your company's name fresh in the client or prospect's mind, even when you're not in front of them or on the phone with them.

Let's face it, you can't be calling people every day, every week, or even every month. It's not just annoying, but it's a waste of their time, and more importantly, it's a waste of your time. Besides, you're going to run out of things to speak about. On top of that, there will be clients who will start avoiding your calls if they believe the only reason you ever call is to try and sell them something.

Persistence Follow-Up Tips

Here are three good ideas you can implement immediately to keep your name in front of your prospects and clients in a nonthreatening yet beneficial (to both them and you) way. Another benefit of these ideas is that each one gives you a great reason to call.

Newsletters

With the advent of technology and the ease, convenience, and low cost of e-mail, sending out a regular newsletter is now easier than ever. Set up a separate e-mail folder for all your clients and prospects, then one push of the "send" button gets your newsletter delivered. However, if you're going to do this, do it right. Here are some ideas:

- *Don't make it an advertisement for your products or services.* Sure, you should have your contact info and a link to your web site, but the main thrust of your newsletter should be great information that will help your clients and prospects become more successful.

- *Be consistent.* Send out your newsletter on a regular basis. Don't bite off more than you can chew. If you don't think you can come up with something every week or month, send it out quarterly. And it should go out on the same day during these periods. This way, people might actually be expecting it and looking forward to it. I've been sending out a weekly e-mail newsletter for over two years (if you would like to sign up for it, just go to my web log at www.greshes blog.com). On the other hand, my friend Jon Beyle, who is a PE teacher and high school coach, also runs an athletic training and fitness business for high school athletes. He sends out his newsletter on fitness tips quarterly. As long as it's consistent, it doesn't matter how often.

- *Keep it short and simple.* About 250 to 500 words is sufficient. Remember, you want people to read it, not admire it. The HTML format looks great and if you choose to do it, fine, but text format will work for you too. Besides, far too often, HTML gets picked up as spam. The key is not how fancy it is, but how good the information is.

By the way, newsletters are another good excuse for calling clients and prospects. "Hi, just wanted to make sure you've been receiving our newsletters. How do you like them?"

Newspaper and Magazine Articles

Find out what your clients and prospects are interested in; find articles on these subjects, cut them out, and mail them with a handwritten note that states, "Thought you might be interested in this." You can also do this with articles pertaining to their company or industry. The great thing about this is, aside from doing something nice, you now have a reason to call. "Hi, did you get the article I sent you?" You've given yourself an opening to discuss business.

Seminars

This is not only a great way to keep you in front of your clients and prospects in a positive way, it's also a great way to sell and an even better way to make yourself indispensable to your clients, which is something you'll see more of in later chapters. Like the newsletters, the seminar content should not be an infomercial, but should be something that will help the attendees become more successful in either their business or personal lives. You're creating value by giving them something they can't get from your competition. You can do this with a big budget, as many large companies do, or you can do it in a very cost-effective manner like many small businesses do.

For example, Bridgestone/Firestone Tires of North America does most of its business through a dealer network of approximately 3,000 independent tire dealers. Bridgestone/Firestone, through its management's efforts, has created one of the most loyal dealer networks in the world. In 2005 the president of Bridgestone/Firestone North America, John Gamauf, sponsored me to travel around the country and speak at meetings put on by some of their bigger dealer groups. At these meetings Bridgestone/Firestone managers get up and talk about the company, the new products that are coming out, and any new marketing and advertising campaigns. But the bulk of the meeting is me getting up in front of dealers and dealer personnel, talking to them about how they can increase their business and become even more successful.

And don't think you have to be a Fortune 500 company to do this. The small local law firm that takes care of any of my legal problems runs seminars every once in a while for clients and prospects on things like estate planning or how new tax laws could affect them.

Find a subject that is important to your clients and prospects, and set up a seminar that addresses it. Do a plug for your company, but make the bulk of the program valuable to the audience. By the way, another good reason to call: "Hi, wanted to get your feedback on the seminar. Are there other subjects that would be of interest to you?"

It's a funny thing about life, but life is not a sprint, it's a marathon. To me, that's part of the beauty of life. You see, in order to be successful in a sprint, you have to flat-out win it. But in order to be successful in a marathon, all you have to do is finish.

If you know anyone who runs marathons, you know what I'm talking about. Have you ever asked that person if they won? Come on, no one ever wins those things. It's always some little guy from Ethiopia who wins those things.

But aren't you always impressed when they tell you that they finished? Of course you are, and you know why? Because anyone can finish a sprint. Anyone can last 100 yards. But not everyone has what it takes to hang in there for 26 miles.

The reason that all you have to do is finish in order to be successful is that most of the competition will drop out before the race ever ends. Most of your competition does not have what it takes to go out there day after day after day, because they don't understand that success is not just a one-time thing.

Those salespeople who are successful know it's a lot easier to get to *be* the best than it is to *stay* the best. Most people will relax after that first taste of success, because they don't understand that all the time, energy, effort, and commitment it takes to get to the top are the same things you have to apply every single day just to stay on top. Over the course of the marathon of life, everything you had to do to get to the top, you have to keep doing every day.

We see this happen with market leaders all the time. I call it "the responsibility of being number one." Being number one—whether it means being number one in your marketplace or industry, or even being the number one salesperson in your company—is a real good news/bad news proposition.

The good news, of course, is you're number one and it sure beats being anything else. The bad news, however, is you're number one, and that means you walk around with a big red bull's-eye on your back. You are the person or company that everyone is shooting at. You are the Super Bowl on everybody's schedule. Let's face it, if you beat everyone out for a sale or client, who cares? You're number one, you're supposed to. But if *they* beat *you* out—whoa, let's pop the champagne corks, it's time to celebrate.

The problem for the company or person who is number one is they have no one to shoot at, and they can develop a tendency to get complacent. Why do you think most championship sports teams never repeat as champions? First of all, their goal was simply to reach the top. Repeating what they've already achieved doesn't necessarily carry the same sense of excitement or urgency. Plus, once you're the champion, everybody wants to beat you and has more incentive to play just a little harder against you than they do against anyone else.

The big problem with complacency is that the goal of the competition is to get where *you* are. If you are satisfied where you are and your attitude is, "We're doing fine. We're number one. We've earned it. We can relax a little now," you give your competitors the opening to catch you. And once they catch you, they can certainly pass you.

However, if you are constantly striving, as a company or individual, to be better at who you are and what you do, if you are always pushing ahead and looking to move forward, it won't matter if your competition gets to where you are, because at that point, it will only be where you used to be.

To best sum up the power of persistence, I'd like to pass on to you a story that was told to me many years ago by my father-in-law, Charlie Romano (I had to mention his name, otherwise he'd be demanding royalties). It is a story that has been passed on in many different scenarios.

This is a story of a man who possessed a tremendous amount of commitment, desire, and persistence—lucky for him, too, because he didn't have much of anything else. He had no job, no money, and he had a family to support. What he wanted more than anything was to work. He wanted a job and he was willing to do anything. He looked every day and he looked everywhere, but he just couldn't connect.

Finally, as a last resort, he went to see his parish priest. He said to him, "Father, can you help me? I will do anything to support my family. Can you please help me find a job?" The Father looked at him and said, "I'm glad you came here, because I can help you and I will. My best friend is the president of New York University. I will give you a letter of recommendation. Take it, go see him, and I'm sure he can help you find a job."

This guy was thrilled. He took the letter of recommendation, thanked the priest, and headed on down to NYU. He met with the president of the university, showed him the Father's letter, and told him his story of how he was out of work, had no money, and had a family to support. He said to the president, "I will take any kind of job. Will you please help me?"

The president looked at the man and said, "I'm glad you came. I'm glad the Father sent you, because I can help you and I will. I am going to give you a job right here at NYU. I am going to make you the head janitor here at NYU."

Now this guy was just ecstatic. He said, "That's great. Could I start right away?" The president said, "Sure, but just as a formality, would you please fill out this work application?"

When he heard that, this guy's face fell faster than the French army. He looked up and said, "I'm sorry, I can't; you see, I can't read or write."

The president looked at this man and said, "We've got a problem. You must understand I'm the president of a major university. How would it look if I started hiring people who couldn't read or write? I'm terribly sorry, but now I can't help you."

Well, this guy was devastated. He got up to leave. As he was walking out the door, the president said, "Wait, I hate to see you leave empty-handed; here, take this." It was a box of cigars.

The man said, "I don't need that. I don't smoke."

The president said, "Please take it. I'd feel better if you didn't leave empty-handed. It's brand new. The wrapper is still on the box."

So he took the box and left. He started wandering the streets of Manhattan. He ended up downtown in the financial district, standing all alone on a street corner, the box of cigars under his arm.

All of sudden he looked up and across the street he saw a cigar store. He got an idea. He said to himself, "I'll sell that store owner my box of cigars. At least I can make a few dollars."

So he walked into the store and told the store owner his story about how he was out of work, he had no money, had a family to support; but he had this box of cigars, brand new, the wrapper still on it, and would the store owner please buy the box.

The store owner looked at him and said, "I'd love to help you, but I can't. Please understand I've been a reputable store owner for 20 years. How would it look to my customers if I started buying cigars off the street? I'm terribly sorry."

As the man was leaving the store owner said, "Wait minute. I have an idea. There are a lot of people walking around this area with money in their pockets. Why don't you make up a sign, go a few blocks down, and sell the cigars for a dollar apiece?"

The man said, "Do you think I could?" The store owner said, "You could try."

The man said, "Would you help me? I can't read or write. Would you make the sign for me?" The store owner agreed.

The man took the sign, went a few blocks down, put up the sign, put out the cigars, and in *two hours* he sold every single cigar. He had $20 in his pocket. He got another idea. He said, "You know what? I'm going to take this money and buy two boxes of cigars!"

So he took that money and bought two boxes of cigars and sold those. He took that money, bought four boxes of cigars, and sold those. He said, "Whoa, this is great! I'm coming back tomorrow."

Well, he came back the next day, but let's remember, this was a man of commitment, desire, and action. He might not have possessed the highest level of education, but commitment, desire, and action have nothing to do with education.

He was not only back the next day, but he was back day after day, week after week, month after month; he was out on that corner selling those cigars. He was out there for *five years*! It didn't matter if it was hot, cold, rainy, windy, sunny, or snowing, he was out there for *five years*!

Finally, he decided he'd like to get in out of the rain, and he had another good idea. He said to himself, "You know what? I'm going to buy that cigar store."

So he approached the owner and told him the story about the cigars and the corner, the five years, the dollar apiece, and the wind and the rain and the snow, and how he'd like to buy the store. Was the owner willing to sell?

The store owner looked at the man and said, "I've been here twenty-five years now, I'm ready to retire. I'll sell."

The man asked, "How much do you want?" and the store owner replied, "I want a million dollars."

"A million dollars!" the man said. "Where am I going to get a million dollars?"

The store owner said, "Why don't you go to a bank and take out a loan?"

The man said, "Do you think I could?" "Well, you could ask," said the store owner.

So he went to the bank, sat down with the loan officer, and told *him* the story about the cigars and the corner and the five years and the dollar apiece and the wind and the rain and the snow and the store, and he wants to buy the store, so can he take out a loan?

The loan officer said, "How much do you need?"

He answered, "I need a million dollars."

The loan officer said, "That's a pretty big loan. Do you have any collateral?"

The man looked at him as if he had two heads and said, "What? Collateral—what's that? Look, you don't understand, I can't even read or write. What's collateral?"

The loan officer, who by now had written this guy off, said, "Do you have any money?"

The man replied indignantly, "Yes, I have money. In fact, I keep my money in this bank. I don't know how much I have, but here's the bankbook." And he threw the bankbook at the loan officer.

Well, this loan officer opened the bankbook and his hands started to shake; his eyes popped right out of his head and his jaw dropped. He looked up at the man and said, "My God, you have $465,000 in this bank!" He was so amazed he started to repeat himself, "Four hundred sixty-five thousand dollars, $465,000—from selling cigars on a corner for five years! Sir—" (notice all of a sudden he's "Sir") "Sir," he said, "you are a financial genius. And you can't even read or write." He said, "Have you any idea where you would be if you could read and write?"

The man said, "Yeah, I'd be the head janitor at NYU!"

10

Your First and Most Important Sale Is at Home

My father gave me the greatest gift anyone could give another person, he believed in me.

—Jim Valvano

At the beginning of 1986 I made the decision that I was going to quit my job and start my own business as a professional speaker and sales trainer. This was really a big step, since I had spent my entire career working for other people. I had been a salesman, sales manager and then division head for an apparel manufacturer in New York City's Garment Center. After 10 years of that I had had enough, so I changed careers and went to work for a sales training and consulting company as head of sales and marketing. After a little more than two years of that, I decided it was time for the big step: my own business.

Upon arriving home that night, I said to my wife, Linda, "I think I'm going to start my own business." Now we had only been married a little over two years and were planning on starting a family in the near future. In addition, we had just bought a larger apartment in our building in Manhattan and had taken on a pretty big mortgage. My timing was not perfect. Most spouses would have reacted in one of the following ways, and I would have been neither shocked nor disappointed if Linda had. What most spouses would have said was:

- "Are you sure this is the right time for such a big step?"
- "You have a good job, and you're doing well, are you certain you want to give all that up?"
- "Maybe we should wait until we've saved more money and can better handle the mortgage."
- "We talked about starting a family, maybe you should wait."
- "Have you given this enough thought?"

Or at least most spouses would ask, "What kind of business do you want to start?"

Well, I'm proud to tell you that Linda didn't say any of those things. All she did was turn to me and say, "It's about time." Now that's what I call inspiration!

We are living in a time when people's lives are not only more hectic than ever, but changing rapidly. The last 30 years have given us:

- The proliferation of the dual paycheck, dual career household (*Fortune* magazine found that 84 percent of two parent households were also two paycheck households).

- The service economy, affordable easy-to-use technology, and corporate downsizing have created thousands of new entrepreneurs and businesses, along with the end of the "I worked for one company my whole life" worker.

- Portable do-it-yourself pensions (the 401k) and soon-to-be-portable health insurance now make it easier for the American worker to change jobs.

What this all means is, it is more critical that ever for spouses, couples, and life partners to:

- Have short- and long-term goals for their lives and careers.

- Share those goals with each other. How can you possibly set a goal and develop a plan for your life, career, or business without including your spouse or partner?

- Have total backing and buy-in of those goals from each other. In business and especially in sales, do you really think there's going to be anyone, besides the people closest to you, who could care less whether you got rejected a hundred times this week? Good luck if you do.

There is nothing worse for a marriage, a life partnership, or even a business partnership than to have two people going off in totally different directions, or a situation where one person doesn't stand 100 percent behind the other in a life-changing decision or venture.

I have seen more marriages and relationships ruined or severely strained because one person didn't fully believe in the other, or because the two people were going off in different directions, totally wrapped up in their own lives and issues as if no one else existed. I actually know couples who have separate bank accounts for "his money," and "her money." One of them might be saving up to buy a house, while the other wants to use what they refer to as "my money" to invest in a business. To me, this is insanity. It's just basic, common sense that two people working together toward a common goal will achieve a lot more than two people, who are supposed to be together, going off in opposite directions.

It's virtually impossible for a person to be successful in a new business venture or career without the inspiration and energy someone gets when they know they have total backing at home. I would never have started my business without it.

Let's look at some of the instances that are quite common in today's society where inspiration at home is crucial:

- Starting a new business.
- A career change or new sales position.
- A job transfer to another part of the country.
- Deciding on whether to go back to work or quit a job to stay home and raise children.

When starting a new business or sales job, chances are you're going to have a rough first few years. Every day that you go out in the world as a new business owner or salesperson, be prepared to have your brains beaten out. Rejection will be your constant companion. The last place you need your brains beaten out, or to get rejected, is at home. Home has to be the place where you will get only positive reinforcement. It has to be your safe haven.

We had some very rough years when we first started our business. But whenever I would get down, Linda would invariably come up to me and say, "Just think about all the great stories you're going to be able to tell someday."

I spoke to a young man who had recently embarked on a new career in sales. He told me he enjoyed the work, but his wife wasn't happy that he had to work a lot of nights. This is a typical example of what could be a rewarding career put in jeopardy before it gets started. Where are the shared goals? Where is the realization of shared short-term pain bringing long-term gain?

I told that young man it wasn't his wife's fault that she was complaining about the long hours and the night work. It was his fault for not communicating to her what it would take on a short-term basis for him to be successful in the long term.

One suggestion I made to him was that he should take his wife out with him on some of his evening appointments. This would give her a better idea of what he actually did and how hard he was working. It would also show her that she had a role and a stake in his success.

Sales is not an easy profession, especially in the first few years. The hours are long, the rejection constant, and there could be a good deal of traveling. Not exactly the best prescription for a successful marriage. However, by bringing your spouse into the process, you are giving yourself a much better chance to succeed. I know it worked for me when I started my business.

In my first couple of years in business, I was away from home constantly. I would speak anywhere, whether they were willing to pay me or not, just to get exposure and hopefully generate some paying customers. Linda was at home, taking care of our newborn son, and it was hard on both of us.

One day I decided to take her on a road trip with me so she could get an idea of exactly what I was doing. We drove from New York City to Hartford, Connecticut, where we stayed overnight. The next day I conducted a full-day public seminar I had promoted on my own. After speaking all day, we packed up and headed to New

Haven, where I delivered an after-dinner speech to a group of sales-people. We then got in the car and drove back to New York, arriving around midnight.

The next day Linda said to me, "You spoke all day and night. All I did was sit around, and I'm exhausted. I can't imagine how you feel." This trip not only gave Linda an idea of what I actually do, it also gave her a better understanding of the kind of sacrifice and dedication it was going to take, on both her part and mine. But most importantly, I think it helped her to see that she had as big a stake in the success or failure of our business as I did, even though she wasn't a full-time participant. Ironically enough, Linda now works with me full-time and owns 50 percent of the company.

Just because you know that to succeed in sales means long hours (sometimes nights and weekends), client entertainment, and nights away from home in mediocre to crummy hotels, don't think your spouse automatically knows that. The only time they actually know it for sure is not just when you tell them, but when you show them by making them part of the process.

If you expect total support at home, I don't feel you can ever think in terms of "his" or "hers," or "mine" or "yours." It always has to be "ours." For one spouse to ask another, "When is 'your' business or job going to pay off so that we can live a better life-style?" is demoralizing. There is no inspiration at all in that statement. Once two people make a commitment to each other there can only be "our," because everything that's going on in each other's lives and careers overlaps.

Twenty to thirty years ago, if a husband was offered a better job or a promotion that entailed relocating, it was easy: Sell the house, pack up the family, and go. But it's a little more complicated now. The other spouse is probably working too. That person might have an excellent job or own their own business. At what point is one spouse holding back the other? This is where shared goals and an ability to think long-term come in.

A few years back a close friend of mine was offered a big promotion. The money wasn't that much more, but the responsibility was far greater and his exposure and reputation in the industry would receive a huge boost. The only problem was that it was 200 miles away. His choices were to relocate the family or get an apartment where his new job was and commute between Albany, New York, and eastern Long Island. His wife, realizing what a great opportunity it was, was 100 percent supportive of anything he wanted to do. His children were not crazy about moving, especially his high school–age daughter, which is understandable since that is a tough age for kids to be starting over, but they did fully support him taking this new job.

When they sat down and looked at their short- and long-term goals, they decided that as tiring and disruptive as a 200-mile commute can be, it was the best way to go. They realized this job was a stepping stone that would lead to even bigger and better things within two years, and those bigger and better things would most likely entail relocation. So what my friend chose was short-term pain (the added expense of an apartment to use during the week, and being away from the family at least three to four days a week) for long-term gain.

Naturally, if he felt he was going to spend the rest of his career in this job and location, the family would have moved. But he was only able to make these decisions and have these choices because he had 100 percent backing at home.

I think one of the biggest decisions couples and especially women are wrestling with these days is what to do after the baby is born—stay home or go back to work. It's the kind of decision where full support and shared sacrifice are crucial. It's also the kind of decision, I believe, that people make for all the wrong reasons.

For instance, I've spoken to many women who would like to stay home with the children but decided not to because both the husband and wife felt they couldn't afford to lose that extra paycheck.

In many cases they're right, they can't afford to lose that paycheck, but in plenty of other cases they're wrong. They're just not willing to plan ahead or make the hard choices necessary. A good portion of that extra paycheck goes to the government. Another chunk pays for child care. Then what about clothing, transportation, lunches (at least five dollars a day just for a sandwich and drink), and let's not forget that $3 latte on the way to work. I know people who could have funded their 401(k) plan just on the money they spend at Starbucks.

All of a sudden, living on one paycheck seems a lot more doable. Naturally there is still some belt tightening needed, but this is where the sacrifice and support come into play, in addition to the focused realization of what is truly important.

Many couples say they need that extra money coming in but then end up spending it on everything but the child (bigger house, European vacation, eating out . . .). Then there are the husbands who don't want to lose their wives' paycheck because of the extra pressure it might put on them to earn more, and vice versa.

If a mother or father wants to stay home and raise the children (stay-at-home dads are one of the fastest-growing segments of the population), there is no reason it cannot be accomplished. Of course there are many couples who don't want to give up careers or businesses, and that's fine. The point is, if you really want a lifestyle change, then goal setting, prior planning, a willingness to sacrifice, and a supportive spouse can make it a reality.

Recently I had the opportunity to be the keynote speaker at the annual sales conference of a large food products corporation. I arrived the day before and attended the awards banquet that night. I sat next to a young woman who had just returned to work from maternity leave. The dilemma for her and her husband was that they both believed one of them should be home with their son, but she really enjoys her job. What they decided was that he would stay home and take care of the baby. He restructured his job so that he could work part time, work out of the house, and if he had to go out and see customers, he would do it at night after his wife arrived home.

Linda and I faced this same situation when our son, Michael, was born. We mutually decided, just before Linda got pregnant, that she would quit her job and stay home with the baby. It was both a tough and easy decision—easy in that Linda really wanted to do it and I was all for it; tough, because she was earning good money and I had just started my business less than a year before. How we managed was through smart planning and shared sacrifice.

We knew we had the better part of a year before Linda would give birth and give up her job. We worked like dogs in that time period, earning and saving as much money as we could. We saved over $20,000 in that one year and used it as a cushion for the next year, because whatever I earned would have to support the three of us.

In addition, we sacrificed. No vacations unless it was part of a speech and the client was paying; eating out was cut to a minimum; the BMW was traded in for a Toyota Camry; the living room went unfurnished for a couple of years. We watched every penny. It was not easy—but of course if it were easy, everyone would do it.

Our short-term pain eventually paid off in long-term gain. In four years the business started booming. Because of our sacrifice and our ability to live on one income, Linda was able to come into the business and work with me. This enabled us to not to have to hire and pay someone from the outside, and because we work out of the house, it still allowed Linda or me to be there with the children (our daughter, Emily, was born in 1991).

What made this all possible was three factors:

1. *Shared goals.* Both Linda and I felt strongly that one of us should stay home with the children. This enabled us to easily sacrifice material possessions to achieve that goal.

2. *The ability to think long-term.* We both knew a few years of up-front sacrifice would reward us with many, many more years of long-term rewards and allow us to exert much more control over our lives.

3. *Total spousal support.* Linda sacrificed a lot of short-term material pleasure not just to be a full-time mother, but in the hopes that the business would grow. Never once during the lean times did she question the business's existence, nor did she ever say I should get a job and give up. She had as much if not more confidence in my ability as I had, and knew there was no way we would not be successful. That's true inspiration, the kind everyone needs.

11 | Successful Salespeople Sell More than Just the Product or Service

The only way to know how customers see your business is to look at it through their eyes.

—Daniel R. Scroggin

Over the last 10 years, no matter what industry or company I walk into, whenever I ask executives or business owners to tell me the biggest issues they face in the marketplace, by a wide margin, two answers rise right to the top:

1. How do we differentiate ourselves from the competition?
2. How do we consistently create and sell value rather than get stuck selling price?

In these next four chapters, you'll learn what successful salespeople are doing to overcome these issues.

THE ELEVENTH ROCK SOLID RULE FOR ACHIEVING SALES SUCCESS
Successful Salespeople sell more than just the product or service.

Successful salespeople understand what it is that they really sell, because, first and foremost, they understand who the customer is and what they really want.

You don't have to be a genius to know that the world is changing, and changing rapidly. Because of globalization, advances in technology, the Internet, and free trade, the business world of today is more competitive than it's ever been in its entire history.

Think back 25 to 30 years ago and you'll find entire countries such as China, India, South Korea, Singapore, Taiwan, the Czech Republic, and Ireland, whose economies barely registered a blip on the radar screen, that are now anywhere from thriving to major powers in the world's marketplace.

Hell, there are huge companies out there that either didn't exist 25 to 30 years ago or were too insignificant to even bother about. Think of Intel, Microsoft, Dell, Southwest Airlines, Geico, and Wal-Mart. These companies are not just market leaders, they're giants.

You're probably wondering, "Is there a point to this?" Yeah, there is—in fact, two points. One, you never know where your next big competitor is going to come from, so you better be aware of everyone. That guy working out of his garage today (just like Steve Jobs) could be eating your lunch a few years from now.

Twenty-five or 30 years ago, who was Wal-Mart? Basically, it was a guy, Sam Walton, who was putting up stores in small out-of-the-way towns where no other retailer wanted to be. Do you think 30 years ago Sears considered Wal-Mart competition? The funny thing is, 30 years later, do you think Wal-Mart considers Sears competition?

If you don't believe that this can happen to almost anyone or any company, consider the mess at General Motors. In the 1950s and early 1960s the saying was: "What's good for General Motors is good for U.S.A." That's how much a part of the fabric of this country GM was.

Of course, back then there was little or no competition since World War II had destroyed the manufacturing infrastructure of so many other countries while leaving the United States intact.

Back in the 1970s GM's U.S. car and truck market share reached 48 percent; today it has declined to half of that. They grew fat and lazy.

Their board of directors consists mainly of former CEOs who took other companies down the tubes. They continue to proliferate brands (Pontiac and Buick) that just drag down the bottom line. Most of all, they missed the boat on innovation time and time again.

The latest example is hybrid-electric power systems. Toyota and Honda pioneered this innovation while GM just scoffed. GM executives told the Detroit press that only environmental thumb-suckers would find such vehicles appealing. They completely misread the situation.

Now we have hybrid vehicles for which there are long waiting lists and for which customers pay full list price or even higher. Yet GM will not have any hybrids until 2007—if then.

If it can happen to them, it can happen to you.

Some companies are so asleep, they won't wake up till it's time to go back to sleep. To this day, the legacy (actually *dinosaur* is a better name) airlines still believe the only reason Southwest Airlines and JetBlue are wiping up the floor with them is strictly because of price. As you'll see in the next chapter, nothing could be farther from the truth.

The second point is this: The age of doing business by accident is over. Clients and customers have so many choices today that you can't expect to just show up, throw your briefcase on the table, and grab an order.

Now, is this a doom-and-gloom scenario, stating that there's no more opportunity out there? Of course not. In fact, there's more opportunity out there today than ever before. I really believe, and I'm going to show you why over the next four chapters, that no matter how successful you are right now, you have an opportunity to be more successful than you've ever been before.

There's just one catch: In today's competitive world there is no more margin for error. The companies and the people that will succeed today, tomorrow, and on into the future are the ones who will be willing to do everything right.

I know that as a client, customer, or consumer I can buy almost anything I want from the Internet and I never have to talk to you! So the question now becomes, what is it that you are willing to do for all your clients, customers, and prospects that creates so much extra value that it is more beneficial for them to buy directly from you than to just click on their computers?

In other words, how are you differentiating yourself from the competition?

I think the single biggest question I have for you is this: *What are you really selling?*

Are you just selling whatever will get you the fastest commission, or are you selling extraordinary quality, service, convenience, and value? Are you just selling the first thing out of your bag, just to get your boss off your back, or are you selling "Save me time and make my life easier"? Are you just selling whatever the *customer* thinks they want and need, or are you selling knowledge, expertise, information, and education?

Are you just selling stuff? Are you just selling what everyone else is selling? Because if you are, I can click on my computer and I can buy stuff from the cheapest guy in town—and if you're bothering to read this book, I know that's not you.

Do you know who really makes it hard for the top 10 percent of all salespeople who are truly successful? The 90 percent who aren't. In far too many cases, their actions have created a perception of the great salesperson as someone who is a "slick talker," or a fast-talking, joke-a-minute character who can talk you into anything.

Now granted, a lot of perceptions are created by Hollywood. The con man is glorified. Herb Tarlick of the old TV show *WKRP in Cincinnati* is depicted as a "born salesman," when, in fact, he's an incompetent idiot.

But no matter how these perceptions are created or where they come from, most of the responsibility for them falls right into the lap of every salesperson out there.

I want you to read this e-mail I received from one of my radio show listeners.

I am an eye doctor in California and have to say the word "sales" to me has a negative connotation. If I was to be set up on a blind (hate to use the word while at work) date with a woman who is a saleswoman, I would have too many negative traits that would come to mind and would have to refuse the date. I work in a LASIK clinic and would recommend the term excite with education. I tell them the features of our clinic and how the surgery would benefit them and I am 100% honest and up front with them and their questions. I find patients respond to this and appreciate not being SOLD the procedure but being educated about it to the point they are excited to move forward with no hidden agenda other than to make their lives better. From this moment forward can you use the term Excitement Educators????

Your thoughts?

Dr. Jason Cavanaugh

Now, I have to admit, when I first read this e-mail, as someone who has been in sales for over 30 years, I was insulted by it. I immediately thought of all the bad doctors I've come across in my life—especially the doctor who told my mother the pain in her abdomen was all in her head, and it turned out to be ovarian cancer. But then I thought of all the good doctors I've met, like the doctors who cured my dad of colon cancer and performed successful quadruple bypass surgery on my father-in-law.

The point is, every profession breaks down the same way: 10 percent are great, 10 percent are awful, and the other 80 percent are totally average. Whose fault is it that Dr. Cavanaugh feels the way he does about salespeople? I would have to guess it's probably the fault of the salespeople he has dealt with over the years. If he ever met a great salesperson, there's a real good chance his perceptions would change.

What's ironic is that, from the way Dr. Cavanaugh described how he works with a patient (he tells them the features and benefits, is 100 percent honest and up front, educates the customer), little does he realize, this is what a successful salesperson does. I have seen it done many times.

Successful salespeople find out what a client needs and make sure they get it all the time. It goes beyond selling the client what they want, because far too often what they want is not what they need. Here is where too many salespeople get in trouble. They are so desperate to close a sale and so afraid the client will say no, they take the point of least resistance and let the client buy whatever they want, even if the salesperson knows it's the wrong thing.

A successful salesperson would rather turn down a sale than sell a client something she knows won't fill the client's needs. Let's be honest: If a client buys what they insist they want and it turns out to be something they didn't need, do you think they're going to call that salesperson and say, "Listen, it's not your fault. I insisted on buying this. So don't worry, from now on I'm going to listen to you." Yeah, right, and chicken have lips.

No matter whose fault it is, as the salesperson, as the one who is supposed to have the knowledge, I've got news for you: It's your fault. Clients expect salespeople to tell them what they need. Otherwise, what do they need them for?

Clients also expect salespeople to make it easy for them to buy. In a world where time has, in many cases, become a more valuable commodity than money, the most successful companies and salespeople are the ones who are the easiest to do business with.

If this were 20 or 30 years ago, when people's lives weren't quite as stressed, you could make it a little more difficult for clients to do business with you and they might overlook it or work through it. But not today; there are too many choices. Make it the least bit difficult for me to buy from you and I'm gone.

When my wife and I relocated our family to North Carolina in 1997, there was a lot of preparation involved and a lot of hassles. Finding a mover, renting a house (we planned on building, but didn't want to do it till we were living there), canceling phone service in New York and turning it on in Chapel Hill—the list goes on and on.

One of the tasks that turned out to be easy was finding a new bank for both my business and personal accounts. It was made easier because of the efforts of one salesperson. Her name is Jane Sturdivant and at the time (she is since retired), she was working for Branch Banking and Trust (BB&T). I know this sounds surprising to you, since bankers are notorious for being poor salespeople, but Jane was definitely an exception.

I called three banks in Chapel Hill to see which one I wanted to work with. The first bank took forever to get back to me, and when they finally did, I found myself speaking to someone who couldn't have been much older than 14, who really wasn't very capable of answering my questions.

With the second bank I spoke to somebody right away. He didn't ask one question about my business, but he was very anxious to send me a brochure outlining all the different accounts, along with the fees and conditions under which they operate. Do they think anyone ever reads that crap? Besides, who has the time? What I needed was someone who could tell me everything I needed to know, so I wouldn't have to waste time reading a stupid brochure.

On the third call I found someone who was willing to do exactly that. Jane asked me numerous questions about my business and personal life. She wanted to make sure the accounts I opened would fill my needs. There were no papers to fill out; Jane did that for me. All I had to do was send the bank a check to put in the account and sign the account papers.

In addition, when she found out that we were planning to build a house within a year or two after moving, she got the ball rolling by introducing me to the bank's construction loan and mortgage specialist not long after we moved.

On the afternoon of July 1, 1997, we drove into downtown Chapel Hill. The first stop we made was the local BB&T branch. When we walked in the door, Jane had both my business and personal checkbooks ready. My checks had cleared and there was money in the accounts. She handed me a box of deposit slips, and 30 minutes after arriving in town, I was in business.

Successful salespeople aren't a certain personality type. You don't need to be outgoing to be honest, hard-working, focused, informed, and persistent. You don't need to be funny to make sure a client's needs are filled on a continuous basis, or to do more than you're supposed to do.

Time for a sales rant.

I've always noticed that the most successful salespeople always do more than they're supposed to do. They never do the minimum. Now this is not something that takes extraordinary talent or ability, yet most salespeople—heck, most people—don't do it. I always wondered why, and I think one of the main reasons is that in school the concept of doing more than you're supposed to do, or going the extra mile, is not something that is taught as being valuable. Of course, most people who work in public school systems don't do it, so why should they teach it?

As you can tell, I'm not a big lover of school. Don't get me wrong, I think education is not just important, it's critical. However, far too often, school doesn't have a hell of a lot to do with education. There are far too many public school systems in the United States that are nothing more than jobs programs for the marginally employable.

In school we're taught that if you do what you're supposed to do when you're supposed to do it, you'll get an A. Unfortunately, in the real world, doing what you're supposed to do when you're supposed to do it gets you a C, which places you squarely in that middle 80 percent. Maybe that's why selling more than just the product or service, while not a skill that's hard to acquire, seems so rare.

12

Successful Salespeople Create and Deliver Value and Don't Sell Price

Price is what you pay. Value is what you get.

—Warren Buffett

As a professional speaker, I have a huge edge on many of my clients: I don't speak in only one industry. I speak in a wide variety of industries to a wide variety of companies. One of the many things I enjoy about what I do is that I get to learn about all these different industries and companies. I also get to see what goes on in these industries and their marketplaces. Let me tell you what I see going on in almost every single industry and marketplace that I have walked into in the last 5 to 10 years.

The middle is dead! The middle is gone!

If you want to be successful in today's business world and economy, you have to be one of two things: the cheapest or the best.

The days are long gone when you could sell a pretty good product or pretty good service at a pretty good price, because I can get "pretty good" at a dirt cheap price. Or I can get "fantastic" at just a little more expensive price, because pretty good just isn't good enough anymore.

Look around you, go to any shopping mall. Look at the stores that do business and look at the stores that do not. On the one hand, you have your deep discounters, such as Wal-Mart, Target, and Kohl's. But even down at this end, where price is supposedly the deciding factor, how do you explain what happened to Kmart? Similar merchandise, similar prices, but not nearly the same results as Wal-Mart, Target, or Kohl's.

Walk into a Wal-Mart, Target, or Kohl's and you'll find them well lit (you could use a pair of sunglasses in Wal-Mart) and well stocked. I don't know about you, but I've walked into quite a few Kmarts that were poorly lit, and let me tell you something about poor lighting. When a store is poorly lit it looks dingy. When it looks dingy, it can look dirty, even if it's clean.

Another thing I noticed in Kmart are what's known as "holes in the shelves." This is a retailing term signifying they're out of that item, causing a big empty space on the shelf (hence the term). Now I don't know about you, but for me the biggest reason to go to a large discounter like Wal-Mart is that I don't have to worry they won't have what I'm looking for, since they seem to have everything. With time becoming such a precious commodity in people's lives, do you really think people want to shop somewhere that won't have what they're looking for and they'll have to go somewhere else? So even down at the price end there's a value component.

Let's look at the other side of the coin from the cheapest—let's go to the best. These are retail stores like Nordstrom, Saks Fifth Avenue, Neiman Marcus, Lord & Taylor, along with specialty operations like Banana Republic and Abercrombie and Fitch.

Then right in the middle you have those mid-range, mid-price department stores. You remember those places. Your mother used to drag you there as a kid. Thirty years ago every major city in America had at least three or four of them, and now maybe one or two are left. They either went out of business, merged, or were taken over.

What made the department stores great in their heyday was personal service. Once the discounters started to flex their muscles by cutting price, the department stores started to do the same. The problem was, in order to cut their price, they had to cut somewhere else, and where do you think that was? That's right, they got rid of the people who provided personal service.

The customers responded predictably. They figured as long as they were going to get abused, they might as well go to a discounter and pay less for the privilege.

✍ SALES TIP

You don't compete on what your competition does best and you don't. You compete on what you do best and they don't.

So here it is: You have to be the cheapest or the best. The question is, where do you want to be? Well, if you want my advice, I'll tell you where you never want to be. You never want to be the cheapest. You never want to be known as the "price company" or the "price salesperson."

THE TWELFTH ROCK-SOLID RULE FOR ACHIEVING SALES SUCCESS

Successful salespeople consistently create and sell value, rather than get stuck selling price.

Let's look at three reasons why you shouldn't want to sell price.

Price Is Easy to Duplicate

Price is, without a doubt, the single easiest thing for the competition to duplicate. Any idiot can drop their price. It doesn't take a genius to do that. The toughest things for the competition to duplicate are extraordinary quality, service, convenience, and value, because extraordinary quality, service, convenience, and value require the most effort. And you know as well as I do that most people and most companies are not willing to put forth extra effort. And do you know why? Because it's hard! But let me tell you what I tell my kids every time they come to me and say, "But Dad, we can't do this, it's too hard." The funny thing is, I have no idea why they keep saying this, because they already know how I'm going to answer (maybe they're hoping I'll forget). I'll just turn to them and say, "Yeah, I know it's hard, and you know why it's hard? Because if it were easy everyone would do it."

But you see, it's the "hard" that makes you great. It's the willingness to do the hard that makes you great. It's the willingness to do the hard that will separate you from the competition, because most of them are only willing to do the easy and drop their price.

In 2000 I had the opportunity to be the keynote speaker for National Sporting Goods Association's annual meeting. To help me prepare for my speech, the association sent me a research paper they had put together about the sporting goods industry. It covered the decade of the 1990s. At the end they had come up with 10 conclusions. One of them jumped off the page at me. It stated that in the 1990s, every sporting goods chain whose primary marketing strategy was to sell price went out of business.

Now when it comes to selling price, I'll make one compromise. There's only one thing selling price could be good for: getting someone to try your product or service the first time. However, price is never something that keeps them coming back. I also think this is better as a retail strategy than in a business-to-business situation (see the accompanying Sales Tip for explanation).

When Japanese auto manufacturers first started selling cars in America, you might recall they were cheap. In fact, they were cheaper than American cars, but that was part of the strategy. The Japanese knew they had a good product, but they needed people to buy the cars and agree with them. Once the customers started buying the cars and seeing how reliable they were, they kept coming back. Of course, the price started to rise, and now Japanese cars are quite a bit more expensive than American cars.

About six months ago I was sitting in my office when my phone rang. It was a cold solicitation call from an insurance agent. The name of the company will remain anonymous to protect the stupid.

The young man at the other end of the phone said, "Mr. Greshes, I'd like to speak to you about long-term care insurance."

I told him, "I already have long-term care insurance," and he asked, "Who do you have it from?"

I answered, "Northwestern Mutual." He immediately said, "You know, we're cheaper."

Instantly, I decided this guy had to be the world's number one idiot. He knew nothing about me. He had no idea what kind of policy I have. In fact, it could be the lousiest policy Northwestern Mutual sells (it's not). But right away he knew he's cheaper.

I responded by saying, "I have a really great agent," which is 100 percent true. (By the way, if you're wondering why I didn't just hang up on this guy, it's because I knew that this would make a great story.) My insurance agent is not someone who just sells me policies. He is, as you'll find out later in the book, my expert, adviser, and resource.

What this young man said next just blew me away. He said, "Oh, he's your friend." Amazing: Now I knew he wasn't the biggest idiot in the world; he was the second biggest. The biggest idiot was whoever trained him. This young agent was led to believe there were only two reasons why anyone would buy from an insurance agent:

1. His products were the cheapest.
2. The client was his buddy.

Now, I will tell you, my agent is not my friend. Don't get me wrong—I really like him. He's a good guy, but we never socialize. I buy from him because he's great at what he does and he constantly does the right thing for my family and me. He fills our needs on a consistent basis. Our relationship has nothing to do with price.

✍ SALES TIP

The strategy of enticing people to buy for the first time by lowering your price could be dangerous, depending on what you're selling. There's an old saying we used to use in the garment center: "The way you break them in is the way they're always going to be." Meaning if you're cutting your price, right from the beginning, be prepared to do it all the time.

Price Is Not What the Clients Want

What clients really want is extraordinary quality, service, convenience, and value. They want to work with a salesperson who can save them time and make their life easier. But most of all, they want, demand, and need someone who can consistently deliver knowledge, expertise, information, and education, and they're not as worried about price. Yet many clients end up buying price, and do you why? Because they find it so difficult to find all that other stuff. The single biggest reason a client will buy price is that far too often it is the only alternative that we leave them with.

If you want to continue to sell nothing but price, do you know what you'll become? An airline. Now there's a scary thought. There aren't too many industries much dumber than the airline industry. The dinosaur airlines (American, United, Delta, Continental, Northwest, USAir) have done a great job of cannibalizing each other. If they ever wrote a book about the airline industry, it would only have to be one chapter long: Chapter 11.

A few years ago I read a quote from Donald Carty, former CEO of American Airlines. (He was the one who, in the name of fiscal responsibility, forced the workers to take a pay cut while he was handing out big bonuses to the top executives. I guess that was a reward for bringing American to the brink of bankruptcy.) He claimed that the reason the discount airlines like Southwest and JetBlue were taking away so much business from the dinosaur carriers was because of price.

As someone who has been a business traveler for almost 20 years and has flown over 3 million miles on American, plus hundreds of thousands of miles on the other dinosaurs, I can tell you that's a bunch of crap.

The reason the dinosaur airlines are losing market share to Southwest and JetBlue is that even at a lower price, Southwest and JetBlue give you more *value* than the dinosaurs!

At one time I was at the Executive Platinum level on American Airlines. That's their highest elite level. It is essentially two notches above dirt. I was flying 100,000 to 150,000 miles a year on American, mostly on first class tickets. For the past three years, I've done far more flying on Southwest than any other airline, and it wasn't about price. I can prove it: I don't pay for the tickets, my clients do.

I fly Southwest because they do two things better than any other airline I've flown: (1) They leave on time and (2) they land on time. In addition, when you call them they usually answer on the first ring. If you cancel a ticket there's no penalty, and you have a year to reuse the money. However, if it's a full fare ticket, you get a full refund. There's no extra charge for changing your reservation, and their web site is so easy to use, you don't even have to know how to use a computer to book a ticket.

In the three-plus years I've been flying on Southwest, I have never been delayed for equipment trouble and I have never missed a connection. By the way, in case you're wondering, I don't own any Southwest stock, and they are not and have never been a client of mine.

The last time I flew Delta, the flight was cancelled because someone dropped the door as they were closing it and damaged it. There were 50 people on the flight and one gate agent to help us find new flights. They were going to be kind enough to fly me to Boston from Raleigh by way of Atlanta. I told them to stick their ticket, phoned Southwest, within minutes booked a flight to Providence that was leaving within an hour (far cheaper than the Delta flight), rented a car in Providence, and drove to Boston.

I was on an American flight that pulled into the gate at O'Hare airport 15 minutes early and I still missed my connection. Bet you're wondering how that could happen. We sat at the gate for almost 45 minutes because they couldn't get the jetway to work. When I suggested to the flight attendant that they get a step truck, let us off the plane, and then fix their jetway, she said, "Sir, we all have someplace to go."

"Yeah," I said, "but if you don't get where you're going you still get paid—I don't." Needless to say, by the time I got off the plane, my connection was gone.

Hey Mr. Carty, tell me again how the discounters are killing you on price.

Selling Price Makes You Replaceable

Selling price never makes you indispensable to a client; it only makes you highly replaceable. What do you think is easier to find—a salesperson who is willing to cut his price, or a salesperson who acts as an expert, adviser, and resource to his clients? Obviously the price cutter is much easier to find, so why be one of those? If the whole idea is to differentiate yourself from the competition, why not be something that clients can't get enough of: an expert, adviser, and resource.

If you are always delivering extraordinary quality, service, convenience, and value; if you constantly save your clients time and make their lives easier; if you're always making the client better at what they do by giving them knowledge, expertise, information, and education, how can they possibly get rid of you? Do you think someone like that is easy to replace?

Ah, but the price sellers, replacing them is a snap, because no matter how low your price is, someone is going to come along and cut it. There are even companies who will sell at a loss just to steal your business.

In 2004 I was in Las Vegas delivering a keynote speech to 800 independent tire dealers. The client sponsoring the event was American Tire Distributors, the largest tire wholesaler in the United States. The night before my speech I attended a company function where the CEO said to me, "The biggest problem with these dealers is that so many of them still believe the easiest way to sell tires is by cutting your price." Now this is death for an independent dealer since they have to compete with mass merchandisers like Wal-Mart and Sears.

Right after that the CEO then said, "However, many of these people will tell you they have customers who have been with them for years who just walk in, throw their keys on the counter, and walk out."

The next morning I got in front of this audience of 800 independent tire dealers and started off with three questions. First, "How many of you believe that you and your staff know more about tires than the people at Wal-Mart and Sears?" Almost everybody's hand went up. I then asked, "How many of you believe that your dealership can deliver better service than Wal-Mart or Sears?" Again, almost every hand went up. Then, last question, "How many of you believe you can beat Wal-Mart or Sears on price?" Hardly any hands popped up, to which I replied, "You can beat Wal-Mart and Sears in two out of three categories, yet so many of you insist on competing with them in the one category where you can't win."

Then I asked two more questions. First, "Raise your hand if you believe the best way to sell tires is by cutting price." Unfortunately, many hands went up. Next, I asked, "Please raise your hand if you have customers who have been with you for 10 or more years who just walk in, throw their keys on the counter, and leave, because they trust you to do the right thing?" Almost every hand went up.

I then said, "So what you're telling me is that you believe your best customers are morons. Since the best way to sell tires is by cutting price, people who walk in, throw their keys on the counter, and leave without worrying about price must be idiots."

But what it really boiled down to was this: They didn't really believe their best customers were idiots. What they were really saying was, "We'd like more of those long-term loyal customers, but it's easier to cut price than do what it takes to find more of them." Unfortunately, it's only easier in the short term. In the long term, that strategy is going to come back to haunt you.

About nine years ago, I received my greatest lesson in value versus price and the old saying, "You get what you pay for."

As a small business owner with a two person company (my wife and I), I get slammed by the cost of health insurance. About 12 years ago, when we were still living in New York City, tired of rising premiums, I bought a policy with a low premium but high deductible ($2,000). Needless to say, within two years that premium was skyrocketing and the only way to keep it down was to raise the deductible (to $3,000).

One day Linda and I decided this was way too expensive, and we started looking for an alternative. We found a company named HIP, Health Insurance Plan of New York (more like Horrible Insurance Plan of New York). The premium was the same as we were paying but there was no deductible. It was an HMO and you were assigned to an HIP Health Center in your area.

This seemed too good to be true, and I've always been taught that when something seems too good to be true, it usually is. So I did something very smart. Although we signed up the family for HIP, I decided to wait three months before I dropped my other coverage, just in case. It was one of the smartest decisions I ever made.

First, my son had a rash on his hands that wouldn't go away. We took him to the pediatrician at HIP over and over again, but she couldn't seem to diagnose it. Finally, I said to Linda, "You know that dermatologist you used to go to—the one with the diploma. Why don't we just take Michael there and pay the $100 for a visit." Well, we took him there; the doctor took one look and said, "That's eczema," an incredibly common rash among kids. He gave us a prescription and within no time it was gone. Strike one.

Next, I had a terrible pain in my ear. I went to see the general practitioner at HIP. He looked at it and told me to go to the front desk and they'd set up an appointment with an eye, ear, nose, and throat doctor. I went to the front desk, gave them the referral slip, and they said, "Okay, we'll call you." I said, "What do you mean you'll call? When will that be?" They said, "It could be two weeks from now, but we're not sure." I said, "I could be deaf two weeks from now." Finally, after some of my best New York yelling and screaming, I got an appointment for the next day. Strike two.

The capper came when my wife went to see the gynecologist. About a week later she got a prescription in the mail from a doctor she'd never seen, along with a note telling her she had a sexually transmitted disease.

Now follow this: Here's a woman who has just been told she has a sexually transmitted disease, and this same woman has a husband (me) who travels a lot on business. You could only imagine what was going through her mind.

I was not the least bit worried, since my idea of a hot time is ordering room service and watching a night baseball game on ESPN. I told Linda, "You know the gynecologist at NYU you used to see—the one with the diploma from a medical school. Please go see him and pay the $100 for a visit." Of course, she went to see him. He took one look at her and said, "It's nothing." Strike three.

Needless to say we dropped HIP after three months and never again bought health insurance based on price.

Look around you, be observant, learn from companies and salespeople that do it right, but also learn from companies and salespeople that do it wrong. A great example of a company that rose to the top by doing everything right, stumbled because they forgot what got them there, and is now making a huge comeback is McDonald's.

McDonald's is not only number one in its industry (and I don't think there are many industries more competitive than fast food), but they have been number one for many years and they are number one by a mile. They did it by understanding who the customer is and what they really want.

McDonald's corporate motto is Q, S, C, and V: quality, service, convenience, and value. Notice it doesn't read "quality, service, convenience, and cheap" or "quality, service, convenience, and food." The thing that was always so smart about McDonald's was that they advertised price far less than their competition did.

McDonald's ran ad campaigns like "Food, folks and fun"; "Mac tonight"; "We love to see you smile"; and my favorite, "Have you had your break today?" Think about that last one and think about all your clients, customers, and prospects. What do you think they'd rather have, a cheap hamburger or a break? I'm sure they'd rather have a break. McDonald's always seemed to understand what customers really wanted.

In addition, if you have children or grandchildren, I'll bet you've taken them to McDonald's. Here's another question: When you decide where to go with the kids, who really makes the decision? The kids, I'll bet. I know it has nothing to do with you.

That's another thing McDonald's really understood. They realized they had two distinctly different sets of customers: kids and adults. They also were well aware of the fact that different sets of customers quite often buy for totally different reasons.

Now let's go back to when you take your kids out to eat this junk. Tell me if this has ever happened to you. Has one of your kids ever come up to you and said, "Mom, Dad, today let's go to Burger King. I just found out: we can save a quarter!" Has that ever happened? No, and I bet it never will.

The ironic thing about all this is that whenever the kids go to these places, they always get the same thing: a hamburger, French fries, and a Coke. Now as far as I'm concerned, a hamburger, French

✍ SALES TIP

I'm sure many of you reading this book have different sets of customers who buy for totally different reasons. Are you aware of these different sets of customers and have you figured out what makes them buy?

You could be a salesperson working for a company that sells through a dealer network. In that case, your customers are the dealers and the dealers' customers who end up using your products and services. In this case the end user wants a quality product, with quality service, that will do what they need it to do. But what do your dealers want from you? As independent business owners, they're more interested in how you can help them increase their business.

How about if you're a financial adviser working through spheres of influence, like attorneys or accountants? Obviously, you want them to recommend their clients to you. And their clients want a good return on the investments you recommend. But what do the accountant and attorney want? Hey, they want to look like heroes for recommending you.

How about the real estate agent who works with builders, attorneys, and designers, not to mention people buying and selling houses? Well, obviously, people buying a house want the best house they can get at the best price they can afford. The people selling the house want it done as quickly as possible, while also getting as close to the asking price as possible. But how about the builder, attorney, or designer? Well, I'm sure they would love to swap leads with you.

Always understand that you might have different sets of customers and that all these different sets of customers buy for different reasons. It's up to you to figure out what they are.

fries, and a Coke is a hamburger, French fries, and a Coke, and I don't care where you take the kids.

But now McDonald's heard this. They knew people were saying a hamburger, French fries, and a Coke is a hamburger, French fries, and a Coke. But they didn't want people believing that.

That's kind of like saying "A real estate agent is a real estate agent" or "A telephone system is a telephone system. All these companies are the same. All these salespeople are the same." If clients really believe that, then what do you think they're going to buy? Right, price! But like you, McDonald's didn't want to be the cheapest, they wanted to be the best.

McDonald's knew that if all your kids wanted was a hamburger, French fries, and Coke, that would take the decision out of the children's hands, leave it up to you, and you could go anywhere, even to the cheapest place.

So, McDonald's decided they would no longer sell the children a hamburger, French fries, and Coke. Now they sell them a Happy Meal! And do you know what a Happy Meal is? It's a *hamburger, French fries, and a Coke*! Except they give the kids a five-cent toy, stick it in a four-cent box that has puzzles on it, and the kids love it!

Why? Because McDonald's knew—they understood who the customer was and what they really wanted, and they knew *the kids didn't want the food*! The kids wanted the toy, they wanted the box, because kids don't buy food, kids buy fun. They figure they can get food anywhere. Some of them can actually get it at home (if you're laughing you know exactly what I'm talking about).

So what happened was the kids no longer went up to their parents and said, "Mom, Dad, I want a hamburger, French fries, and a Coke," which would leave the decision to you and you could go to the cheapest place. Now they're saying, "Mom, Dad, I want a *Happy Meal*," which leaves you with one choice, McDonald's, and they get all the business by understanding who the customer is and what they really want.

My next question to you is this: What is your happy meal? In other words, what is it that you are willing to do for all your clients, customers, and prospects that no one else is willing to do? How are you differentiating yourself from the competition?

Now let's look at McDonald's other set of customers: adults. I'll bet many of you have eaten at McDonald's without your kids being around. Why did you do it? For the cuisine? I doubt it. I'll bet the single biggest reason you did was because you're a busy person.

You know what happens: You're running around like a chicken with its head cut off. You're trying to bring in new business, service the existing business, your boss is on your back, a crisis erupts, all of a sudden it's lunch time, and you're hungry. You just want to eat and you don't care if it's food (you know what I mean).

So you go to McDonald's because it's fast, easy, clean, and most of all consistent. You know before you ever walk in the door what it will look like, smell like, taste like, cost, and you know you're not going to die—at least not right away. So you go to McDonald's because you are a busy person.

I learned this lesson almost 20 years ago. I was delivering a morning speech in New Haven, Connecticut. I had to give an afternoon speech in South Jersey, about 120 miles away, and I had about 20 minutes to get there.

I got on Interstate 95 and I just started to fly. I was really moving. It was around noon and I hadn't eaten yet that day. I was starving but I didn't have time to stop. All I wanted to do was roll down my window and have someone slap something in my hand that I could shove right in my mouth.

About 20 miles down the road I saw a sign. You'll recognize this kind of sign—I call it a "trick food sign." That's the kind of sign on the highway that states, "Next exit—food."

Have you ever been dumb enough to follow one of those signs? Well, I have. If you've ever gotten off at the exit, when you get to the bottom of the ramp, what do you find? Right, another sign with an arrow that states, "Food."

Ever been dumb enough to follow that sign? Well, if you have (like I have), you'll know you have to go 10 miles out of your way just to get there. Then you have to get out of your car and get the food. Then you have to eat and get back in your car and drive back those 10 miles. But did you ever notice that you can't because there always seems to be a divider in the road? You then have to go another 10 miles out of your way and come back.

It's sort of like driving in New Jersey. You can't take a left in New Jersey. If you miss your turnoff you have to go to Pennsylvania and come back.

Well, I wasn't about to be fooled again so I kept going. About another 20 miles down the road I saw another sign, but this one was a giant billboard in bright orange and yellow colors that said "Mc-Donald's"! And I'll tell you what, it didn't say "cheap" and it didn't say "food," all it said was "easy access off, easy access on." I said, "Damn, how'd they know I was coming."

Because they knew, they understood. They knew who the customer was and what he really wanted, and it had nothing to do with the price.

13 | Successful Salespeople Know What Clients Buy and Why

Too many companies measure what they think is important rather than what the customer feels is important and what they like.

—David Freemantle

In preceding chapters I mentioned that in today's world, time has become a much scarcer and more valuable commodity for many people than money. But how did we get this way, and what has caused this phenomenon?

If we again go back over the past 25 to 30 years and look at the biggest demographic charges in American society, guess what turns out to be the biggest change of all? If you said, "Women in the workplace," give yourself a gold star.

Women in the workplace not only constitute the biggest demographic change in American society over the past 30 years, but they have also had a major impact in most if not all of the leading industrial powers of the world.

The advent of women in the workplace has changed all the rules of the game when it comes to selling. It has changed who the customers are, what they buy, and how they buy, but more importantly, it has changed *why* customers buy—and not just why women buy; it has changed why men buy too.

Think about this: thirty years ago most women were not working; they were at home, raising families. And what did families have a lot more of back then that they pretty much have none of now? That's right, time. People used to get their errands done on a Thursday morning or a Monday afternoon.

Why do you think stores are now open on Sunday and supermarkets are open 24 hours a day? Because people like buying milk at two in the morning? No, it's because they don't have *time*!

Do you know what women used to do a lot more of back then that they don't do nearly as much now or in the same way? No, not cook. It never fails, whenever I ask that question during a speech it's always some guy that says, "Cook." It's also always some guy who looks like he never misses a meal.

But the answer is "shop." Women don't shop like they used to, or as often. Women used to go from store to store to store to store, buying anything they wanted. Sometimes they bought things they didn't want. Why? They had time. They could always go back the next day and return it.

Women don't do that anymore and do you know why? They're busy! They're working. They don't just have jobs, they have careers and they own businesses. Women own 38 percent of all the businesses in America. Those businesses employ 25 percent of all American workers and generate approximately $3 trillion in sales. How has that changed who the customer is?

Boy, it was easy 30 years ago if you were in sales. You walked into a company and asked the first woman you saw if she could tell the boss you were here. Try that now and see what happens.

And don't think it's only in the United States. In Canada, according to a report from the Prime Minister's Task Force on Women Entrepreneurs, there are more than 821,000 women entrepreneurs who contribute more than $18 billion a year to the Canadian economy. Women hold ownership in 45 percent of Canada's small to midsize companies and represent one-third of all self-employed Canadians—more than in any other country.

In the United States, according to the Center for Women's Business Research, among $1 million–plus firms, women are more likely to have started their businesses (73 percent) than are men (60 percent), rather than having purchased, inherited, or acquired them in some other way.

There are more women in law school and medical school than men, and on the undergraduate level, the ratio of women to men is fast approaching 3 to 2. So, for all of you guys out there who couldn't get a date in college, now's your chance—go back.

But what this has created is an entire society of two paycheck households. In fact, according to *Fortune* magazine, of all the two parent households in America, 84 percent are also two paycheck households, and women are the primary breadwinners in 45 percent of these households. In fact, women are the primary breadwinners in 55 percent of all American households, pointing out another huge demographic change: single parent households.

You have millions of families with money coming in from two different places, which means for many of them, money is not the biggest issue. However, since they're both working, while also having family responsibilities, time is now the big issue.

THE THIRTEENTH ROCK-SOLID RULE FOR ACHIEVING SALES SUCCESS

Successful salespeople understand that speed and ease are the two biggest benefits you can deliver to a customer.

These people are your clients; they're your prospects. They're stressed out at work and stressed out at home. The last person they're going to allow to stress them out is someone who is trying to sell them something.

What are you doing to save these people time and make their lives easier? What are you doing to take the fear, stress, and anxiety out of the buying and selling process?

If your clients own their own business they're probably working 12-hour days, six days a week. If your clients work for a large corporation, they probably have a job that five or six years ago included two or three responsibilities. Now, after a couple of rounds of downsizing, rightsizing, reorganization, or just plain firings, that same job has seven or eight responsibilities. Do you really think they want to work with a salesperson who is going to waste their time?

Let's not forget, when I say "your clients," I just don't mean women, but men too. More and more we're seeing responsibilities overlap. Thirty years ago it was easy. Women stayed home and took care of house stuff and kids' stuff; men went to work and took care of work stuff. Now it's all overlapping. In fact, one of the single fastest growing demographic groups in the United States is stay-at-home dads.

Go to any sports stadium in America and you'll find diaper changing tables in the men's room. There are changing tables in the men's rooms at Yankee Stadium! Of course, there's probably a drunk sleeping on them, but that's beside the point.

If you put a gun to my head and said to me, "From now on, you're only allowed to sell two benefits to any client," I would say, "No sweat." Speed and ease: Get it for them as fast as possible and make it hassle-free, and you'll have a client for life.

Saving them time and making their life easier are the greatest benefits you can deliver to a client in today's world. If you don't believe me, let's take a look at the average family's day.

These people wake up in the morning, get dressed and have to get to work. But wait—you also have to wake the kids and make sure they get dressed, eat breakfast, and get off to school. And guess what? Kids don't come home from school at 2:00 or 3:00 in the afternoon anymore—there's no one home.

So they go to day care or babysitting, an after-school program, or maybe to one of the thousands of activities we sign them up for. There are nine-year-olds running around with BlackBerrys.

If you don't think the world has changed, try this one on for size: When I was in elementary school back in the late 1950s, early 1960s, I used to come home for *lunch*! Every kid in my class went home for lunch. Everyone's mother was home. Some kids even got a hot lunch—not me, but some did.

That doesn't happen anymore. By the time these kids get picked up it could be 5:30 or 6:00 at night, and now you have to feed them. Here's another interesting statistic: Fleming Foods, a former client, and, at one time one of the largest food wholesalers in the world, told me that 1996 was the first year in American history that restaurants did more business than supermarkets and food stores combined!

What does that tell you about what people want? Are they worried about price, or are they more concerned about speed and ease? At the local supermarket nowadays, what is one of the most profitable and more popular categories? Prepared meals, of course—but did you also know that *Consumer Report* surveys show the reason people buy them is more for the convenience than for the taste? (I guess that good Styrofoam flavor isn't going over too well.)

As a concession to the changing times, an article in the *Wall Street Journal* about two years ago stated that because of today's time crunch and how meals are now prepared, making Hamburger Helper is now considered cooking. Hamburger Helper—when I was a kid, that was considered dog food; now it's cooking. In fact, the article stated that anything that needed a pot was now considered cooking.

Back to our average family's day. After the kids get picked up and fed, now you have to get them home, make sure they do their homework, and then finally send them off to bed. By the time these parents have a chance to relax it's 9:30 or 10:00 at night. Wow, I really feel like speaking to a salesperson now!

I know that as a client or a consumer, I much prefer to buy from companies that make it as easy as possible for me to do business with them. As a matter of fact, I have a policy about buying and it's this: if you want to sell me something, I do nothing. If I have to help you do any part of your job in order for you to sell me something, I want to split the commission, because I already have a job and don't need another one—especially one I don't get paid for.

The most successful salespeople and companies are constantly striving to create a hassle-free buying experience for their clients. As an example, for the past 15-plus years we've bought almost all of our office supplies from a company in the Midwest aptly named Reliable.

They send us catalogues and we order via their toll-free number. The people that handle the incoming calls are not only courteous but knowledgeable. The orders are handled promptly, then shipped promptly, and the quality is excellent.

Could I honestly say they never screw up? Of course not, everybody screws up. But the difference is how you handle the screw-ups. With Reliable, there are no excuses, no "I'm sorry, there's nothing we can do about it." (By the way, when someone tells you "There's nothing we can do about it," what they're really saying is, "I don't feel like doing anything about it," or, "I don't have enough clout to do anything about it and I don't want to bother the manager," because there is always something that can be done.) If Reliable ships the wrong item, they take it back, no questions asked (they also send a prepaid shipping sticker, contact the shipper for you, and arrange to have it picked up).

If it's something they don't want to take back, they just say, "Keep it at no charge and we will send you the correct item." They understand that the biggest fear people have of buying online or from a toll-free number is the fear of being sent the wrong item and not having any recourse. Reliable takes away that fear.

Furthermore, there's a Staples only two miles from my front door. We would still rather deal with Reliable. They have better salespeople (if you can even find one at Staples) and the whole process is so much more hassle-free.

The whole concept of selling speed and ease has even filtered down to products that have always been considered commodities. Look at how gasoline is sold. Years ago oil companies would advertise octane. I always wondered, "What the hell is octane?" Do people really sit around discussing how much octane they're getting? "Hey, I got 93 the other day, how about you?" Who cares?

But now have you noticed how gasoline is sold? Pump, pay, and go; speedpass—get me in, get me out, and get me going. I don't know about you, but I won't buy gas from any station that makes me walk inside.

A better illustration of this was an ad campaign Shell ran a few years ago. It was called "Moving at the Speed of Life." In it you see a woman, dressed in a red business suit, pulling up to a gas pump in an SUV. She swipes her card, fills the tank and she's off—a busy person "moving at the speed of life."

Notice, to get their point across about the benefits of speed and ease, they used the busiest person in the world, a working mother (business suit plus SUV can only add up to working mother).

We live in a time when people are more stressed out than ever before. We spend more time at work than we ever have, yet our family demands are greater than they've ever been. Our kids are exposed to more crap and bad influences than at any time in history and the fact that so few parents are around to supervise them only adds to the stress and worry.

Because of medical science, people are living longer but not necessarily healthier lives. This has created a generation of baby boomers who not only have kids to take care of but elderly parents too. More stress and more demands on their time.

Divorces along with second, third, and fourth marriages have created combined families where the kids literally have four to six sets of grandparents. There are men and women who have inherited kids from two or three other families, bringing along all the emotional baggage with them.

Now you might agree or disagree with all this. You might find nothing wrong with it or you may feel like the world has gone berserk and is coming to an end. But I'm telling you that as salespeople, it doesn't matter what you think. This is the reality of what your clients are dealing with, which means this is what you need to be dealing with, too. If you can't save them time, make their lives easier, and take the fear, stress, and anxiety out of the buying and selling process, they don't need you.

14

Successful Salespeople Are Experts, Advisers, and Resources

The Internet is doing to salespeople what automation started doing to the factory floor over twenty years ago: it's getting rid of the unskilled.

—Warren Greshes

don't like making guarantees. I've been asked by clients if I would guarantee that what I speak about will work. I always reply, "Only if you'll guarantee your people will do everything I tell them to do, every single day."

But I will make one guarantee in this book: I guarantee there is not a single client, customer, or prospect who wants to be an expert on what it is that you do. That's what we have you for: to be our expert, adviser, and resource.

Your clients do not have the time nor the inclination to be an expert on what it is that you do. Heck, most clients don't have the time to keep up with all the information they need to be experts in their own field, let alone yours. That's why your ability to supply your clients with knowledge, expertise, information, and education is critical to not only your success, but theirs, too.

THE FOURTEENTH ROCK-SOLID RULE FOR ACHIEVING SALES SUCCESS

Successful salespeople act as experts, advisers, and resources to their clients, always ready to provide them with knowledge, expertise, information, and education.

As an expert, adviser, and resource, your job goes way beyond supplying your clients with great products and great service. Your job is also to provide the client with the knowledge, expertise, information, and education they need to be more successful in their career or business.

If you can do that on a consistent basis, you will have differentiated yourself from the competition, created so much extra value that your price almost becomes immaterial, and reached the zenith of success in sales: You will have made yourself indispensable to the client.

THE FIFTEENTH ROCK-SOLID RULE FOR ACHIEVING SALES SUCCESS
Successful salespeople are indispensable to their clients.

For example, I've done a lot of work with salespeople in the cable TV advertising business. Many of their clients are local small businesses. These are the kind of businesses that don't have an ad agency representing them and are not big enough to have their own advertising or marketing department.

The most successful cable TV advertising salespeople I've met don't just sell ads to these businesses; they lend their knowledge and expertise to these clients while acting as the client's advertising and marketing consultant.

These successful salespeople first find out everything they can about their client's business. Then, rather than just selling them an ad or series of ads, they help the client formulate an advertising and marketing plan designed to help them get the biggest bang for their ad dollar and, consequently, increase the client's business.

By the way, if you haven't figured it out yet, when you increase a client's business it not only makes you indispensable, but it gives the client the wherewithal to buy even more from you. Talk about a win–win.

Pharmaceutical salespeople have a real tough job. First of all, they have to sell to doctors. That in itself is difficult. Doctors are the kind of people who speak to you as they're walking backwards. If you've ever been in a doctor's office, you know the appointments are stacked up like firewood. Trying to get a doctor to stop for a sales pitch is extremely difficult. The average pharmaceutical salesperson has 2.5 minutes—maybe.

Since the average sales call is 2.5 minutes, this means that some salespeople are getting 5 to 10 minutes and some might be getting only 1 minute. What can you do to make sure you're a 10-minute salesperson rather than a 1-minute salesperson?

Pharmaceutical salespeople don't actually sell the drugs to doctors. They're only trying to get the doctors to prescribe their drug to their patients. How does a pharmaceutical salesperson become valuable to a doctor? By acting as that doctor's expert, adviser, and resource, of course—but how?

We've already established that most doctors' offices are busy almost to the point of insanity. But, through it all, doctors still need to stay abreast of all the latest discoveries and advances in medical science. It has to be almost impossible to keep up with all the reading. Successful pharmaceutical salespeople will not just show up with a brochure or a sales pitch touting their drugs, but with useful information that doctors need in order to stay informed, whether it be the results of the latest clinical trials or findings recently released regarding an important research project. Even if your information saves that doctor only 30 minutes of reading, that still makes you more valuable than your competition.

The Internet is a wonderful invention. I'm amazed at what can be accomplished on the Internet. It gives the little guy a chance to compete with the big boys. I can send out thousands of weekly newsletters with just the push of a button. I can broadcast my radio show over the Internet to listeners all over the world. I can produce broadcast-quality podcasts in my office, upload them to my blog, enabling thousands of people to subscribe to them online through iTunes, Google, Yahoo!, and many other sites. The Internet is one of the greatest inventions of the twentieth century and I thank God that Al Gore invented it.

However, there is one big problem with the Internet: It just throws information at you. That, however, brings me to another big problem. Do you know what most salespeople do? That's right—they just throw information at you.

Here is my challenge to you. If you want to be successful in the twenty-first century, you have to be better than my computer. If you cannot be better than my computer, then I don't need you. You need to be able to take that information for me, organize it, act upon it, and deliver it to me in a way that I can understand it quickly and easily and implement it quickly and easily. If you can't or won't do that, you can be replaced by the Internet or an 800 number.

Right now, the Internet is doing to salespeople what automation started doing to the factory floor in the early 1980s: It's getting rid of the unskilled. But if you remember what happened then, you'll recall that what looked like a bad thing in the 1980s actually turned out to be just the opposite, and that's what I believe will happen here.

Back in the early 1980s the "Chicken Little, Sky is Falling Society" was busy trying to convince us that all this change was bad because we would no longer manufacture anything in America. They told us the Japanese economy would soon blow right past us. We were told that even though the new service economy was creating millions of new jobs, these were low-paying, dead-end jobs. If you remember back that far, the quote from these geniuses was, "We are becoming a nation of hamburger flippers."

Well, here we are more than 20 years later and the results are that we now manufacture more in the United States than we ever have, but we do it more efficiently and with fewer people. The Japanese economy not only never caught us but got left in the dust. Those new service jobs helped spawn the greatest and longest expansion of the U.S. economy, with new vibrant industries (cell phones, biotech, Internet services) and companies (Silicon Valley) springing up all over the place.

The people who are still on the factory floor are more highly educated than ever, more highly skilled than ever, more highly in demand than ever, and because of that, more highly paid than ever.

This same thing is happening to salespeople right now and will continue to happen. Those salespeople who continue to throw information at their clients and prospects and who are more interested in closing a sale than developing a client will continue to be expendable.

✍ SALES TIP

Something I haven't gotten to yet but I feel must be addressed is the difference between a sale and a client. A sale is a one-shot deal, but a client is someone who buys over and over again. The successful expert, adviser, and resource is much more interested in developing a long-term client relationship than just closing a sale.

As I wrote in Chapter 11, the stumbling block for far too many salespeople is that they do so little business, they become desperate. Whenever they do get in front of a prospect, they need to close a sale so badly, they'll sell anything, whether the prospect needs it or not. Great, you've closed a sale, but all you created was a short-term, one-shot deal.

A client is someone who buys over and over and recommends other people do the same.

A client is also someone to whom you are selling commensurate with their ability to buy.

For example, let's say you work in the sales department for a large hotel/convention center and you sell corporate travel and meetings services. You have two clients. The first is Harry's Hock Shops, a small chain of pawn shops. They have a couple of meetings a year and spend about $20,000 a year on corporate travel. Of that, they spend about $15,000 a year at your facility.

The second client is the Gigundo Corporation, an international conglomerate with offices all over the world. They have meetings constantly and spend about $10 million a year on corporate travel. Of that they do about $100,000 a year with you. Which one of these is the client?

Obviously, Harry's Hock Shops—you're capturing 75 percent of their budget every year. It's plain to see that, as a vendor, you're extremely important to them and, I'm sure, difficult to replace.

On the other hand, don't even believe for a second that the Gigundo Corporation is a client. You own 1 percent of their business. They threw you a bone to get you off the phone or out of their offices. In the garment center we would call that a "Rachmunes order," a Yiddish expression for what is otherwise known as a "pity order." You can easily be replaced.

And please don't tell me about the "potential" of the Gigundo Corporation. Potential is only good if there's a better than 50 percent chance of you cashing in on it. Until that time exists, they are not a client.

In the year 2000, I was asked to keynote a conference for a large financial services company. Their sales force consists of thousands of advisers, but my audience was only going to be the top 50 producers in the entire company. They were being taken, along with a guest, to Monte Carlo as a reward for their performance.

The day before my speech, I was talking with my contact at this company, and she said to me, "Our business analysts are telling us that in the twenty-first century there will be no more need for face-to-face salespeople." The first thing I thought of was, "If you really believe that, why go through the expense and trouble of bringing these people all the way to Monte Carlo?"

However, I replied, "I only agree halfway with that. I believe," I continued, "in the twenty-first century there will be no more need for poor to mediocre face-to-face salespeople. I believe the Internet will get rid of them."

I said this because every survey on customer buying preferences that I've ever seen tells me that clients still want to buy from a person. Clients still want that personal touch. Even beyond that, however, they want to deal with a person who will be their expert, adviser, and resource while also being a single point of contact that can answer every question or, if they can't, immediately knows of someone else who can.

Clients want someone who will handle their problems for them and not just point us in the right direction (usually into customer service hell). We don't want to be told, "Just call this number and ask for _____." No, we want someone who says, "Give me all the information and I'll straighten it out for you," or, "Tell me what you're looking for and even though I don't do that, I probably know someone else in our company that does and I'll put her in touch with you."

Let me show you what I'm talking about. My current life insurance agent, Don, is not just an expert, adviser, and resource, but he's also a great example of a single point of contact.

Around mid-2004, I had once again had it with my health insurance plan. The premiums were sky-rocketing, and the company's customer service was crap. It was time for a change.

I had been reading about the new Health Savings Accounts that President Bush and Congress passed into law in late 2003. Because these plans were so new the information was hard to find, and it was even harder to find a company who was selling them. What I could find out about these plans made me feel like this was the best solution for a small business owner.

Now even though he does not sell health insurance, I called Don. I knew that even if he didn't sell the product or know anything about it, he probably knew someone who did and who could answer all my questions.

So I spoke to Don, told him what I was looking for, and the next day he faxed me 35 pages of information about Health Savings Accounts along with a note that said, "Read this and if you still feel this is for you, contact me."

Now, you might be saying to yourself, "Thirty-five pages! Doesn't sound like he did much except send you everything he had." Well, think again, and then go to the Internet and tell me how many hundreds, if not thousands of pages of confusing information you find regarding Health Savings Accounts.

I read the information, called Don, and said, "This is exactly what I'm looking for." He said, "Great, I know someone who can handle that for you and I'll put him in touch with you."

He did. A day later I received a call from an agent who specialized in the Health Savings Account product, and within weeks I was all signed up. I made one phone call, not to a salesperson, but to an expert, adviser, and resource who was willing to be my single point of contact.

Extraordinary quality, service, convenience, and value; save me time and make my life easier; give me the knowledge, expertise, information, and education I need to be successful, and give it to me in a way that I can understand and implement quickly and easily; and most of all, be my expert, adviser, and resource who will serve as a single point of contact for me. This is what the twenty-first century customer is demanding.

Yet many clients end up buying off the Internet, calling an 800 number, or just buying price because they can't find enough salespeople willing to be that expert, adviser, and resource. For most of them, it's too hard.

Why do you think women buy more cars over the Internet than men? Most women don't want to go anywhere near an auto dealer because of the way they're treated. They are either ignored, talked down to, or afraid they're going to get ripped off. *Road and Travel* magazine found that women pay 2 percent more for a car than men when they go to an auto dealer.

Whenever I cover this subject with an audience I often ask the women in the audience to talk about their experiences buying a car directly from an auto dealer. Below are the comments I hear most often:

- "Usually the only things they show me are the vanity mirrors and the different color choices."
- "I walked in to buy a new car and I was totally ignored by every salesperson in the place."
- "I was told to come back with my husband." (Some of the women who were told this weren't even married.)
- "I walked in with my husband and they only talked to him." This one really baffles me. Forget everything else; let's just think as logical people. If the husband wants the car and the wife doesn't, no way they're getting the car. Yet if the wife wants the car and the husband doesn't, I've got news for you, they're probably getting the car. So if you must ignore anyone, the odds are, you're far better off ignoring the husband.

Ready for the best part? Women in America make more car buying decisions than men! According to *Road and Travel* magazine, women purchase more than 50 percent of all new vehicles—an $83 billion market. Women spend $300 billion annually on used car sales, maintenance, repairs, and service. Female buyers are the fastest growing segment of new and used car buyers today. Seems to me the only people who don't know this are the yutzes selling the cars!

If you are willing to be an expert, adviser, and resource to your clients and prospects, I honestly believe that right now, no matter how successful you are, no matter how successful you've been in the past, you have the opportunity to be more successful than you've ever been in your entire career. The laws of economics tell us that's true.

The clients are showing us that demand for experts, advisers, and resources is high, yet the supply is low. You don't have to be a member of MENSA to figure out that when demand for anything is high and supply low, whoa, talk about a unique opportunity!

Extraordinary quality, service, convenience, and value; save me time and make my life easier; speed and ease; knowledge, expertise, information, and education delivered by a single point of contact who will serve as my expert, adviser, and resource. This is what the customer of the twenty-first century is demanding and so this is what the successful salesperson of the twenty-first century must be able to deliver.

15 | Successful Salespeople Love What They Do

Success is not the key to happiness. Happiness is the key to success. If you love what you are doing, you will be successful.

—Albert Schweitzer

One of the things I love most about being a professional speaker is that I get to meet and talk to a lot of successful people. I love to hear their stories of how they started and how they got to where they are. To me, the incredible stories of their journeys are far more interesting than hearing how successful they are now.

If I were to think of all the things I've learned from these successful people, two stand out above all the rest.

The first is this: There is no "by the book" way of being successful. Don't let anyone tell you, "You have to do it this way." Even this book—I'm not saying that you have to listen to and do everything I tell you to do. All I'm saying is, here are the things successful salespeople and businesspeople do to be successful. If what you're doing is working 100 percent to your satisfaction, keep doing it. You'd have to be nuts to stop.

But if what you're doing is not working 100 percent to your satisfaction, here are some proven ideas, so give it a shot. What do you have to lose? By the way, if what you're doing is not working 100 percent to your satisfaction and you're not willing to try something different; then you do lose.

There are always going to be people who will tell you, "You *have* to do it this way." Usually they say that because that's the way they do it. But that doesn't mean it's going to work for you. What I've learned from successful people is be yourself. Take advantage and maximize those things that you do well and minimize those things you don't do well, while at the same time trying to improve them.

When I first started speaking, I received a call from another speaker who had listened to one of my audiotapes, and while she thought I had talent and ability, she suggested that I might want to try and get rid of my New York accent. She said it would pigeonhole me as a regional speaker and stop me from being hired in other regions of the country, if not the world.

I thought about this for approximately five seconds and told her that while there might be some people who would not hire me because of a prejudice against how I sound, I didn't care. After all, I didn't need everyone to hire me (just like you don't need everyone to buy from you). At that time my goal was to deliver 100 talks a year (now it's 50). If everyone except 100 companies turned me down, I'd be a happy guy.

Besides, I told her, if I get rid of my New York accent, I'll sound like everyone else, and then how do I differentiate myself—meaning, why should they hire me?

On top of that, if there's a company out there who's looking for an in-your-face, no-holds-barred New Yorker to kick ass and inspire their sales force, they're going to have to hire me, because everyone else will have gotten rid of that annoying New York accent.

In case you're wondering, over the last 20 years, I've addressed audiences in almost every state in the United States, plus audiences in Mexico, the Caribbean, England, Ireland, Wales, France, Singapore, Malaysia, and Hong Kong. Amazingly enough, everyone seemed to understand what I was talking about.

Actually, it was just before my first speaking engagement in the United Kingdom where I learned another lesson about being yourself and finding what works for you.

Almost everyone I told about my speaking engagement in the United Kingdom had this advice: "You know, the British are a lot more reserved than Americans. You better tone down your act when you speak there." I'm sure you have probably gathered from reading this book that my style is high energy and not too subtle. In fact, I'm about as subtle as a punch in the face, and in the world of heart attacks I'm known as a carrier.

However, the "experts" actually had me thinking that maybe they were right, so I called my client in the United Kingdom and asked him. He said, "I hired you because I wanted a high-energy, in-your-face speaker. If I wanted a reserved speaker, I would have hired someone from here." Good point. Be yourself.

The second important lesson I've learned, over the years from all the successful people I've met, also happens to be the one common denominator I've found among all of them. It is also the sixteenth and final rock-solid rule for achieving sales success.

THE SIXTEENTH ROCK-SOLID RULE FOR ACHIEVING SALES SUCCESS

Successful salespeople absolutely, positively love what they do.

The single, biggest reason they do what they do is because they love it. For successful people, there is nothing else they would rather do. Successful salespeople believe that what they do helps the people they do it for, because successful salespeople do not sell, they help. Their attitude is: I cannot help you unless I get to see you, and I certainly can't help you unless you buy something from me.

One of the many things that distinguish successful salespeople from the rest is they believe that what they do and what their company does is the best. Because of that, they believe it is their obligation to make sure the client buys from them. Successful salespeople feel that if they allow a client to buy from the competition, they have done them a horrible disservice by allowing them to buy second-best.

If you want to be successful in sales, in business, or in life, you better love what you do. *If you don't love what you're doing, you ought to get out!* Because I'll tell you this, if you want to be successful, if you want to be great, you have to be willing to put in the time, energy, effort, and commitment to be great. But if you don't love what you do, there's no way you'll be willing to put in that time, energy, effort, or commitment.

If you recall, in Chapter 10, I wrote that when starting in a new sales career or territory, or when starting a business, the first few years are bound to be rough until you build up your client base. I wrote if you didn't have total backing at home it would be hard. Well, let me tell you what's going to make it even harder: if you don't love what you do.

In any new sales career, territory, or business, I can tell you from experience, the last thing that you're going to see is money. There will be some lean times while you are attempting to grow your business. The worst reason to get into sales or start a business is money.

When I ask, "Why did you get into sales," or "Why did you go into this kind of business," I've had way too many people say, "Because I heard you can make a lot of money in sales," or, "I heard you can make a lot of money in this kind of business."

I know people who have made a lot of money doing things that others would turn up their noses at.

You've probably never heard of a man named Randy Repass. He was like so many other people in that he had a job he was disappointed with at a Silicon Valley technology firm, so he turned to his love of boating for relief from the cold, impersonal nature of the high-tech industry. In 1968, working out of his garage in Sunnyvale, California, he began selling nylon rope by mail order under the name West Coast Ropes. Occasionally, adventuresome customers would even drop by to pick up their orders in person.

"I decided from the beginning that I wanted to take care of people," says Repass. "The high-tech industry didn't provide me with an effective way to do that. But the boating industry gave me the opportunity to really enjoy my work and interact with customers who shared my interests. I was having a blast and building a business at the same time."

Repass also saw an opportunity to improve the way people shopped for boating supplies. According to Repass, he was frustrated by the experience of shopping in local chandleries for the parts he needed to outfit his modest day-sailer. "Boat supply stores in those days were usually dark, disorganized places staffed by a couple of salty but indifferent clerks who preferred swapping sea stories with one another to helping customers find what they came in to buy."

Repass's dissatisfaction led him to open the first West Coast Ropes store in Palo Alto, California, in 1975. From that one store, a love of boating and a commitment to helping rather than selling enabled Randy Repass to build West Coast Ropes into West Marine, the world's largest boating supply retailer.

I'm sure that selling tires for a living doesn't seem like the road to riches or the coolest way to make a living, but don't tell that to Paul Zurcher.

Mr. Zurcher (I don't think I've ever called him Paul, and even though he's one of the most genuine people I've ever met, I don't really think I could) left the Armed Forces right after serving in World War II. Having grown up on a farm in rural Indiana, the only thing he knew was that he didn't want to be a farmer.

With the help of a $2,500 loan from a local businessman who took a liking to him and believed in him, Mr. Zurcher bought a one bay service station. As his business grew, he branched out into selling tires. Treating every customer as special (as every customer is), his tire business grew and today Zurcher Tires, more commonly known as "Best One," is one of the largest retailers and wholesalers of tires in the United States, with stores all over Indiana and the Midwest.

Mr. Zurcher, now in his 80s, is as active in the business as ever. While he certainly doesn't have to be—his sons, along with other family members and executives, do a great job of running the company—he loves being there as much today as he did 60 years ago.

You know what? You can make a lot of money doing anything, if you really love it and put everything you've got into it.

Loving what you do is what is going to get you through the hard times when there is no money coming in. It is also the one quality that can help make you great at anything you do.

You know as well as I do, in order to be truly great at something you have to do it all time, day after day after day. If you don't enjoy doing it, do you really think you're going to be willing to do it every day?

I have a friend who quit his job in corporate America, took his buyout, and decided to start his own franchise business. He did extensive research and decided to sign up with a franchisor in an industry that he thought had great potential for making money. The only problem was, it was a business he had no real passion for.

✍ SALES TIP

If you want to be successful in sales, you will find that passion is far more important than experience. There are a lot of salespeople with experience who have either lost the passion for what they do, or never had it to begin with.

As with attitude and commitment, discussed in Chapter 1, clients and prospects get excited and inspired by salespeople with a passion for what they do and what they sell. Besides, if you have a passion for what you do, you'll make sure to do everything you can to gain the knowledge and experience you need.

My friend's business lasted a year. He decided to close the doors because, he said, he was "tired of throwing good money after bad." Now, normally, giving your business a year to be successful is not a very reasonable amount of time. In most cases it can take five years for a new business to make it. However, in my friend's case, he had no passion for the business and industry he was in, so throwing in the towel was probably the smartest thing he could have done.

Loving what you do is probably the single best piece of advice I can give to anyone looking to start a new business or career. Almost 20 years ago, just as I was starting my business, I happened to be watching Oprah on television. The subject of the show that day was female entrepreneurs. There were four women on the show who had started and built successful businesses.

I don't remember any of their names, but I do remember the advice given by one of these successful women. She said, "If you're going to start your own business, find something you love doing and do it all the time, even if you have to give it away for nothing."

Mrs. Fields of Mrs. Fields Cookies started her business exactly that way. She was a housewife who enjoyed baking cookies. Her friends kept telling her that her cookies were so good she should open a store, which she did. However, as I mentioned earlier in this book, just because you build a better mousetrap doesn't mean the world will necessarily beat a path to your door.

Mrs. Fields felt she had built a better mousetrap. She knew that anyone who tasted her cookies loved them, which gave her an idea. She didn't need to sell the cookies, she just needed people to taste them and they would sell themselves. And that's what she did.

She took a tray of cookies, walked out into the mall concourse, and started giving them away. Naturally, people loved the cookies and wanted to know where they could buy more. What a coincidence, she just happened to have a store full of them.

As I noted earlier, I started my speaking business with a marketing plan that stated "I will speak anywhere, anytime, to any group, for any price. Even if you don't want to pay, I'll still show up." I really believed I had something important to say, and I knew if I could only get businesspeople to hear me someone would hire me, and pay me, to speak to their company—which is exactly what happened.

I'm amazed when speakers who are just starting out, and are not exactly busy, tell me they don't want to speak for free. I wonder if they really have a passion for what they do. If they did, they would want to be doing it all the time. Besides, you would think they would rather speak for free than sit in their offices doing nothing for free.

You're probably saying, "Hold it a second. I don't own my own business, I work for a company and can't be giving stuff away for free." Why not? If you really believe your product or service is so great that whoever tries it wants more, then isn't the whole idea to get people to try it?

If you were selling Mercedes-Benzes, would you really have to sell them? Wouldn't it just be easier to give them away for a day or two? "Here, take it home with you, keep it for the weekend. If you like it, buy it, and if not, just give it back."

Can you imagine taking this car home, leaving it in the driveway, showing it to all your friends, and then giving it back? Try explaining that one to your friends next weekend when they want to know what happened to the Mercedes.

Sure, if you're selling something like financial products, you're not going to start giving away mutual funds or stocks, but don't tell me there isn't something, some service or accommodation, you can do for a potential client that will make them want more from you.

In fact, I'd rather give something away than cut my price on it. Once you cut your price, clients are going to expect you to do it over and over again. Very few people are going to expect to keep getting something for nothing.

When I speak I'm often asked, "What would you like to see happen after you're gone? If the audience could take away one thing with them, what would you want that to be?" I always answer that question the same way: I want them walking out of there saying, "Man, that guy really loves doing that." I want them walking out of there also saying, "Wow, no one had more fun in that room than Warren did."

The biggest reason I do what I do is that I love it. It's fun. Sometimes, I stand on a stage and I think to myself, "My God, people pay me to fly all over the world and say anything I feel like saying." When I was a kid, I used to get beat up for doing that. Now they pay me.

But then people always want to know why that's the one thing I want my audience to take away with them. You see, I know if my audience really believes that I love what I do, then they'll be much more likely to listen to what I have to say. If they're much more likely to listen, they'll be much more likely to believe it. If they believe it, they just might give it a shot and act on some of the ideas and solutions I give them. If they do, I'll know it'll work—they'll be more successful, and that is really my true reward.

When your clients, customers, and prospects really believe that you love what you do, well guess what? They'll be much more likely to listen to what you have to say. And you know if they're much more likely to listen to you, they might be more likely to believe you. If they believe you, they, too, might give it a shot and buy something from you. If they do, being a successful salesperson who helps rather than sells, you know it will work for them because it's exactly what they want and need, which means they'll continue to buy from you, and that is your true reward.

Why do we do this? Why do we go out there, even on the days when we don't feel like being there?—because I know no matter how successful you are, you have those days. We do it because we have a commitment to our companies, our clients, our employees, our families; but most of all we have a commitment to ourselves. It states that if we are going to go out there every day and accept compensation for what we do, then we're going to try to be the best we can be.

I would like to end by posing one last question to help you determine if you really love what you do. If you were walking along the beach and you found a magic lamp in the sand, picked it up, rubbed it, and a genie popped out, and that genie said to you, "I am going to give you one big wish. I am going to allow you to do anything with your life that you choose to do," would you look that genie right in the eye and say, "Genie, get back in that lamp, because I'm already doing it!"

Index